MISTER MEZZO

AMERICAN

ILLUST RATION

AMERICAN ILLUSTRATION NINE

THE NINTH ANNUAL OF AMERICAN EDITORIAL

BOOK, ADVERTISING, POSTER, PROMOTION

ART, MAPS AND CHARTS, UNPUBLISHED

WORK AND FILM ANIMATION.

BRAND

EDITOR: EDWARD BOOTH-CLIBBORN **PROJECT DIRECTOR:** BONNIE CLAEYS

DESIGNER: CHRISTOPHER AUSTOPCHUK **ASSISTANT DESIGNER:** RISA ZAITSCHEK

ASSOCIATE WRITER: MARY YEUNG. **SPECIAL THANKS TO** THE SCHOOL OF VISUAL ARTS FOR PROVIDING THE SPACE AND EQUIPMENT FOR THE ANNUAL AMERICAN ILLUSTRATION JUDGING. THE

INTRODUCTION BY EDWARD BOOTH-CLIBBORN **THE JURY** JUDIE ANDERSON, CAROL CARSON, JANET FROELICH, ALEXANDER ISLEY,

BROCHURES, RECORD ALBUM COVERS, AND SELF-PROMOTION **MAPS & CHARTS** MAPS AND CHARTS FOR MAGAZINES

AGENCIES, COPYWRITERS, AND CLIENTS

PRODUCTS, INSTITUTIONS, AND SPECIAL EVENTS **PROMOTION** ILLUSTRATIVE WORK FOR

PUBLICATIONS, PUBLISHERS, DESIGN GROUPS, ADVERTISING

AND ADDRESSES OF CONTRIBUTING ARTISTS, NAMES OF DESIGNERS, ART DIRECTORS,

FICTION BOOKS **ADVERTISING** ILLUSTRATIONS USED IN ADVERTISING **POSTERS** POSTER ILLUSTRATIONS FOR CONSUMER

INTERNOS BOOKS, COLVILLE ROAD, LONDON W3 8BL, ENGLAND.

NEW YORK, NY 10016 **DIRECT MAIL, WORLD:**

TRADE FOR THE REST OF THE WORLD: HEARST BOOKS INTERNATIONAL, 105 MADISON AVENUE,

HAVE BEEN SUPPLIED BY THE ENTRANTS. WHILE EVERY EFFORT

CAPTION INFORMATION IN THIS BOOK

ARTWORK AND THE

HAS BEEN MADE TO ENSURE ACCURACY. AMERICAN ILLUSTRATION, INC. DOES

NOT UNDER ANY CIRCUMSTANCES ACCEPT ANY RESPONSIBILITY FOR ERRORS OR OMISSIONS. IF YOU ARE A PRACTICING

ILLUSTRATOR, ARTIST, OR STUDENT AND WOULD LIKE TO SUBMIT WORK

TO THE NEXT ANNUAL COMPETITION, WRITE TO: AMERICAN ILLUSTRATION,

INC. 49 EAST 21ST STREET NEW YORK, NY 10010, (212) 979-4500. DISTRIBUTED IN THE UNITED

STATES AND CANADA BY: RIZZOLI INTERNATIONAL

PUBLICATIONS 300 PARK AVENUE SOUTH, NEW

YORK, NY 10010 ISBN 0-8478-5571-6. BOOK TRADE

IN UNITED KINGDOM BY: INTERNOS BOOKS, COLVILLE ROAD, 1 LONDON

W3 8BL ENGLAND BOOK

JOHN C. JAY, JEFFREY KEYTON, MELANIE NISSEN, ANTHONY RUSSELL, STEVEN TWIGGER **EDITORIAL** ILLUSTRATIONS

CREATED FOR USE IN NEWSPAPERS AND THEIR SUPPLEMENTS, AND CONSUMER, TRADE, AND TECHNICAL

AND PROMOTIONAL USE **UNPUBLISHED WORK** COMMISSIONED BUT UNPUBLISHED ILLUSTRATIONS

AND PERSONAL WORK PRODUCED BY PROFESSIONALS AND STUDENTS

ANIMATION FILM ANIMATION FOR TELEVISION, ADVERTISING, AND PUBLIC SERVICE **INDEX** NAMES

MAGAZINES AND PERIODICALS **BOOKS** COVER AND INTERIOR ILLUSTRATIONS FOR ALL TYPES OF FICTION AND NON

INTRODUCTION

AFTER EIGHT YEARS OF AMERICAN ILLUSTRATION, IT'S GOOD TO REPORT THAT THIS ANNUAL IS STILL AS POPULAR AS EVER. INDEED, WE HAD MORE SUBMISSIONS THIS YEAR THAN IN ANY PREVIOUS YEAR. AND A GREATER VARIETY OF WORK TO CHOOSE FROM. SOME OF THE GREAT NAMES OF AMERICAN ILLUSTRATION SUCH AS BRAD HOLLAND AND MARSHALL ARISMAN, HAVE HAD WORK ACCEPTED ONCE AGAIN. EQUALLY, THERE ARE MANY NEW NAMES HERE AND SOME NEW STYLES. FOR ME, THIS IS THE GREAT STRENGTH OF AMERICAN ILLUSTRATION. BY JUDGING EACH ITEM ON ITS MERITS ALONE, WE ARE ALWAYS ABLE TO SPONSOR AND PROMOTE NEW TALENT, AND PUBLISH IT ALONGSIDE THE WORK OF

PRESENT AN ANNUAL

WHICH, YEAR AFTER YEAR, HIGHLIGHTS THE DIFFERENCE BETWEEN EACH NEW CROP OF

IN DOING SO, WE CAN

ESTABLISHED ARTISTS.

ILLUSTRATORS AND THEIR

PREDECESSORS. AND WE CAN CREATE

A NEW ENVIRONMENT IN WHICH THE CROSS-FERTILIZATION

OF IDEAS AND TECHNIQUES CAN—AND OFTEN DOES—BEAR

FRUIT IN NEW APPROACHES.YOU'LL FIND SOME EXAMPLES OF THIS IN OUR SECTION FEATURING PREVIOUSLY

UNPUBLISHED

WORK. AS EVER, I AM

INDEBTED TO OUR JURY FOR THEIR HARD WORK

AND UNSTINTED

ENTHUSIAM FOR

AMERICAN ILLUSTRATION. I'M SURE YOU WILL ENJOY THE IMAGES WE HAVE SELECTED.

THE SOCIETY OF ILLUSTRATORS, COMMUNICATION ARTS, PRINT, AND THE

OF NEWSPAPER DESIGN.

THE SOCIETY

ASSOCIATE DESIGN

DIRECTOR, JUDIE HAS RECEIVED

AWARDS FROM

1987, JANET SERVED AS DEPUTY ART DIRECTOR AT THE NEW

AS

YORK TIMES MAGAZINE.

JUDIE ANDERSON, ILLUSTRATION DIRECTOR, ASSOCIATE DESIGN DIRECTOR,

SHE HAS SERVED AS ILLUSTRATION DIRECTOR

AT THE CHICAGO

OTHER PREVIOUS POSITIONS INCLUDE ART DIRECTOR OF THE DAILY NEWS MAGAZINE, AND SHE WAS ONE OF THE

TRIBUNE, AND MORE RECENTLY, ALSO AS

ARTISTS' GUILD OF CHICAGO.

THE CHICAGO TRIBUNE. STARTING OUT AS A FASHION ILLUSTRATOR, JUDIE

NEW YORK SINCE

ILLUSTRATION STUDIO WITH HER HUSBAND. DRAWING ON THAT EXPERIENCE,

1973. OVER THE YEARS SHE HAS USED HER TALENTS IN VARIOUS POSITIONS AT SCHOLASTIC INC., SAVVY MAGAZINE,

ART DIRECTOR, THE NEW YORK TIMES MAGAZINE. PRIOR TO BECOMING ART DIRECTOR IN MARCH

LATER

FORMED A

FREELANCE

JANET FROELICH,

ANTHONY

RUSSELL, PRESIDENT AND CREATIVE DIRECTOR,

ANTHONY

ALFRED A. KNOPF—ADULT TRADE DIVISION. CAROL HAS WORKED AS A DESIGNER AND ART DIRECTOR IN

ALEXANDER

PRINCIPAL

DESIGNERS

OF THE DAILY NEWS

CAROL CARSON, ART DIRECTOR,

DURING THIS TIME CAROL HAS ALSO SERVED AS AN INSTRUCTOR AT THE SCHOOL OF VISUAL ARTS.

NETWORKS. A WELL -TRAVELLED

TONIGHT PAPER. JANET HAS

MS.MAGAZINE, AND THE TIME INC. MAGAZINE DEVELOPMENT DIVISION.

RECEIVED NUMEROUS AWARDS FROM THE ART DIRECTOR'S CLUB, THE SOCIETY OF PUBLICATION DESIGNERS, AND THE SOCIETY OF NEWSPAPER DESIGN.

JEFFREY KEYTON, DESIGN DIRECTOR, MTV

MELANIE IS A

FREELANCE

ADDITION TO ART DIRECTING AND DESIGNING,

TO ROY ORBISON. PRIOR TO HER CURRENT POSITION SHE WAS A GRAPHIC DESIGNER AT A&M RECORDS, WHERE SHE DESIGNED COVERS FOR

MANY OF

MARLEY

MELANIE HAS ART DIRECTED PACKAGES FOR RECORDING ARTISTS RANGING FROM ZIGGY

TODAY'S TOP

PERFORMERS. IN

RECORDS,

DIRECTOR, VIRGIN RECORDS. SINCE JOINING VIRGIN

WHICH HE OVERSEES,

DIRECTOR, CREATIVE

NISSEN,

HAVE APPEARED IN MUSEUMS

THE SOVIET UNION.

MELANIE

SHOPPING BAGS, THE CREATION OF

WORLD, MOST RECENTLY AS PART OF A U.S. DESIGN EXHIBIT THAT TOURED

AROUND

THE

ADWEEK'S WINNERS. ADVERTISING AGE, AND PICABIA MAGAZINE IN JAPAN. JOHN

OWNS JOHN JAY DESIGN, A CREATIVE CONSULTANCY SERVING CLIENTS IN BOTH THE U.S. AND JAPAN. BLOOMINGDALE'S

ALSO

ANTHONY CAME TO NEW YORK CITY IN 1993 AND SUBSEQUENTLY ESTABLISHED HIS DESIGN OFFICE, SPECIALIZING IN THE PRODUCTION OF IDENTIFICATION PROGRAMS AND PUBLICATIONS. HE IS ALSO A PARTNER IN THE SAN FRANCISCO BASED RUSSELL, HOWRY & ASSOCIATES. BORN AND EDUCATED IN LONDON, RUSSELL & ASSOCIATES. ANTHONY IS A DIRECTOR OF THE AMERICAN INSTITUTE OF GRAPHIC ARTS, ON THE BOARD OF THE SOCIETY OF PUBLICATION DESIGNERS, AND HAS TAUGHT DESIGN AT NEW YORK UNIVERSITY. HE HAS ALSO SHARED HIS CONSIDERABLE CREATIVE TALENTS WITH STUDENTS AS AN INSTRUCTOR AT THE SCHOOL OF VISUAL ARTS. ASSOCIATION. HE HAS ALSO SHARED HIS CONSIDERABLE CREATIVE TALENTS WITH STUDENTS AS AN INSTRUCTOR AT THE SCHOOL OF VISUAL ARTS. BROADCAST DESIGN

STEVEN TWIGGER, ART DIRECTOR, ROD DYER GROUP, INC. STEVEN STARTED HIS CAREER AS GRAPHIC DESIGNER FOR AJ VINES LTD. THEN MOVED ON TO BECOME THE ART DIRECTOR FOR EAST MCFARLAND ADVERTISING, BOTH IN HIS NATIVE LONDON. EMIGRATING TO LOS ANGELES IN 1985, HE JOINED ROD DYER GROUP, INC. AS ART DIRECTOR WORKING ON PROJECTS RANGING FROM CORPORATE IDENTITY PROGRAMS TO VIDEO PRODUCTIONS AND FILM ADVERTISING AND PROMOTION. STEVE'S WORK HAS BEEN IN NUMEROUS NATIONAL AND INTERNATIONAL PUBLICATIONS AND EXHIBITS, INCLUDING D&AD, AIGA, GRAPHIS, AND THE TYPE DIRECTORS CLUB. IN 1989, HE ALSO RECEIVED A SILVER AWARD FROM THE ART DIRECTORS CLUB OF AMERICA.

MTV, IS RESPONSIBLE FOR AN ECLECTIC ARRAY OF PRINT MATERIALS FOR BOTH PROMOTIONAL AND ADVERTISING USES FOR MTV, VH-1, NICKELODEON, AND NICK AT NITE. JEFF

ISLEY, PRESIDENT ALEXANDER ISLEY DESIGN. IN ADDITION TO RUNNING HIS DESIGN FIRM, ALEX SERVES AS ART DIRECTOR FOR BOTH ARCHAEOLOGY MAGAZINE AND THE NEW FORBES FYI. PRIOR TO THAT, HE WAS ART DIRECTOR OF SPY MAGAZINE, FOR WHICH HE WAS AWARDED A GOLD MEDAL FROM THE SOCIETY OF PUBLICATION DESIGNERS. ALEX HAS TAUGHT DESIGN AND TYPOGRAPHY AT THE SCHOOL OF VISUAL ARTS IN NEW YORK AND HAS LECTURED AT BOTH NEW YORK UNIVERSITY AND COLUMBIA SCHOOL OF JOURNALISM. HE IS CURRENTLY ON THE EXECUTIVE COMMITTEE OF THE NEW YORK CHAPTER OF THE AMERICAN INSTITUTE OF GRAPHIC ARTS.

DESIGNER WHO "EUDEMONICALLY" RESIDES

PHOTOGRAPHER. SHE WAS ALSO CO-FOUNDER AND CO-PUBLISHER OF SLASH MAGAZINE.

JOHN C. JAY, SR. VICE PRESIDENT AND CREATIVE DIRECTOR, BLOOMINGDALE'S ADVERTISING AND DESIGN DEPARTMENT. JOHN, NAMED BY AMERICAN PHOTOGRAPHER MAGAZINE AS ONE OF AMERICA'S 60 MOST INFLUENTIAL PEOPLE IN PHOTOGRAPHY, HAS BEEN INDUCTED INTO THE RETAIL ADVERTISING HALL OF FAME AND HAS RECEIVED BOTH GOLD AND SILVER AWARDS FROM THE NEW YORK ART DIRECTOR'S CLUB. HIS WORK HAS BEEN PUBLISHED IN GQ, METROPOLITAN HOME,

PORTRAIT OF MUSICIAN KURT WEILL FOR "THE VOICES OF KURT WEILL." **MEDIUM:** OIL DECEMBER 1989

WOJCHECH WOLYNSKI **ART DIRECTOR:** JUDY GARLAN **WRITER:** LLOYD SCHWARTZ **PUBLICATION:** THE ATLANTIC MONTHLY **PUBLISHING COMPANY:** THE ATLANTIC MONTHLY CO.

WRITER: MIKE SAGER **PUBLICATION:** ROLLING

ART DIRECTOR: FRED WOODWARD

HENRIK DRESCHER/JONATHON ROSEN

GREG SPALENKA **ART DIRECTOR:** JANE PALECEK **WRITER:** CONSTANCE M.

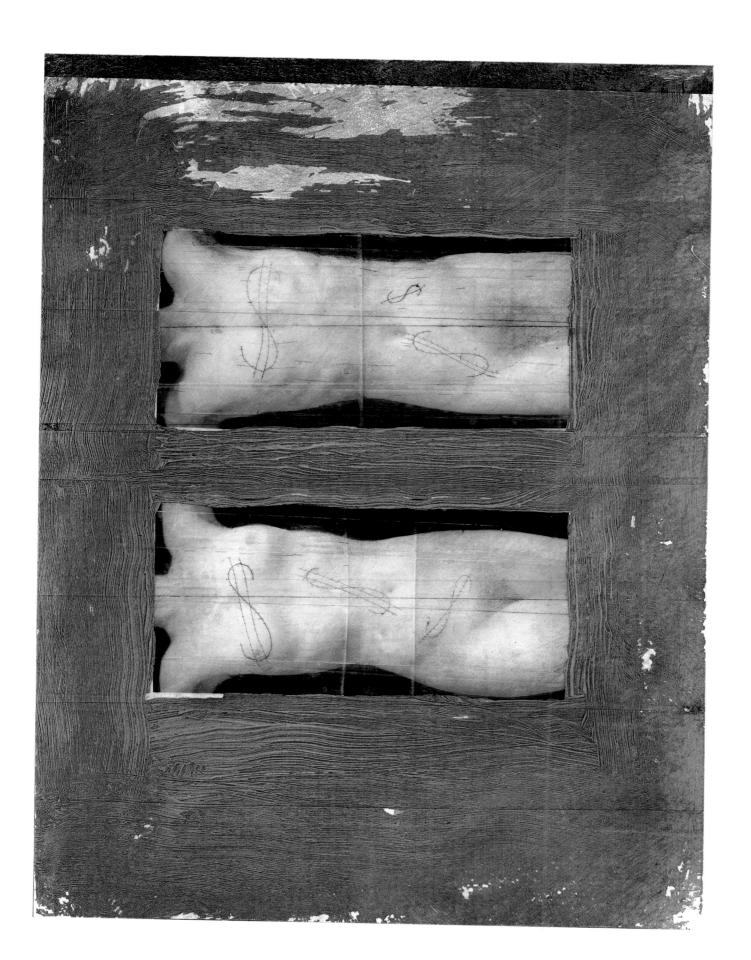

ATION: HIPPOCRATES MAGAZINE **PUBLISHING COMPANY:** HIPPOCRATES PARTNERS INC. ILLUSTRATION FOR A STORY ON WHY HEALTH INSURANCE DOESN'T PAY. **MEDIUM:** MIXED MEDIA DECEMBER 1989

MARSHALL ARISMAN   **ART DIRECTOR:** D.J. STOUT **PUBLICATION:** TEXAS MONTHLY MAGAZINE **PUBLISHING COMPANY:** MEDIATEX COMMUNICATIONS. AN ILLUSTRATION FOR "A CASE OF BLACK AND WHITE," AN ARTICLE ABOUT A BLACK MAN WHO DIED OF UNKNOWN

16

ZOOLOGICAL SOCIETY. AN ILLUSTRATION FOR "SOMEBODY'S KILLING OUR BEARS." **MEDIUM:** OIL ON RAGBOARD JANUARY/FEBRUARY 1990

MARSHALL ARISMAN   **ART DIRECTOR:** GAIL SEGERSTROM **WRITER:** GEORGE NOBBE **PUBLICATION:** WILDLIFE CONSERVATION MAGAZINE **PUBLISHING COMPANY:** NEW YORK

IN HEALTH MAGAZINE **PUBLISHING COMPANY:** HIPPOCRATES PARTNERS INC. ILLUSTRATION FOR THE ARTICLE, "DO YOU NEED A PHYSICAL." **MEDIUM:** PEN AND INK, WATERCOLOR MARCH 1990

PHILIPPE WEISBECKER **ART DIRECTOR:** JANE PALECEK **WRITER:** BENEDICT CAREY **PUBLICATION:**

PHILIPPE WEISBECKER   ART DIRECTOR: SHOSHANNA SOMMER PUBLICATION: ART DIRECTION MAGAZINE PUBLISHING COMPANY: ADVERTISING TRADE PUBLICATIONS INC.   COVER ILLUSTRATION FOR THE JULY '89 ISSUE. MEDIUM: PEN AND INK, WATERCOLOR JULY 1989

PUBLISHING COMPANY: AMERICAN DIABETES ASSOC. INC. ILLUSTRATION FOR THE ARTICLE, "DIABETES, DISABILITIES, AND DISCRIMINATION." **MEDIUM:** INK DECEMBER 1989

20

JOSH GOSFIELD   ART DIRECTOR: PAUL DAVIS DESIGNER: RISA ZAITSCHEK WRITER: RICHARD BAUSCH

PUBLICATION: WIGWAG PUBLISHING COMPANY: WIGWAG MAGAZINE COMPANY, INC. ILLUSTRATION FOR "A KIND OF SIMPLE, HAPPY GRACE," A SHORT STORY ABOUT TWO PRIESTS. MEDIUM: ACRYLIC DECEMBER 1989

WRITER: CARRIE RICKEY **PUBLICATION:** MODEL MAGAZINE **PUBLISHING COMPANY:** FAMILY MEDIA, INC. ILLUSTRATION FOR AN ARTICLE ON NEW MEN IN THE 90'S. **MEDIUM:** MIXED MEDIA JANUARY 1989

"ROCK & ROLL HALL OF FAME." **MEDIUM:** MIXED MEDIA FEBRUARY 1990

JOSH GOSFIELD   **ART DIRECTOR:** FRED WOODWARD   **DESIGNERS:** FRED WOODWARD, GAIL ANDERSON   **PUBLICATION:** ROLLING STONE **PUBLISHING COMPANY:** STRAIGHT ARROW PUBLISHERS. FIVE ILLUSTRATIONS FOR THE SPECIAL FEATURE

25

JOSH GOSFIELD **ART DIRECTOR:** ALAN FORMAN **PUBLICATION:** MANNER VOGUE **PUBLISHING COMPANY:** CONDÉ NAST PUBLICATIONS, INC. AN ILLUSTRATION FOR "MODERNE MANNER," AN ARTICLE ON THE MODERN MAN. **MEDIUM:** OIL 1990

JOSH GOSFIELD   **ART DIRECTOR:** FRED WOODWARD   **WRITER:** KINKY FRIEDMAN   **PUBLICATION:** ROLLING STONE   **PUBLISHING COMPANY:** STRAIGHT ARROW PUBLISHERS. AN ILLUSTRATION FOR "BUDDY HOLLY'S

NAST PUBLICATIONS, INC. ILLUSTRATION

FOR THE ARTICLE, "SEX TEST." **MEDIUM:** ACRYLIC FEBRUARY 1990

31

TOM CURRY **ART DIRECTOR:** ANN KWONG **DESIGNER:** MARGOT FRANKEL **WRITER:** LORRIE MOORE **PUBLICATION:** NEW YORK WOMAN **PUBLISHING COMPANY:** AMERICAN EXPRESS PUBLISHING CORP. AN ILLUSTRATION FOR "VISSI D'ARTE,"

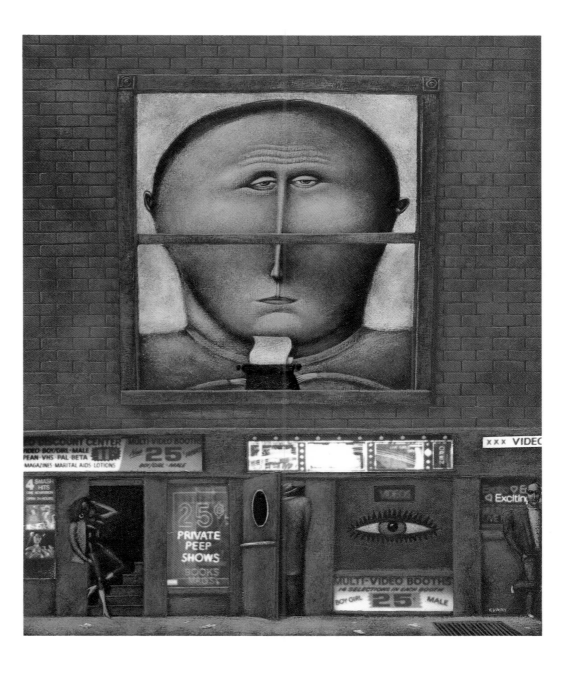

ANITA KUNZ **ART DIRECTOR:** FRED WOODWARD **WRITER:** ALAN D. MAISLEN **PUBLICATION:** ROLLING STONE **PUBLISHING COMPANY:** STRAIGHT ARROW PUBLISHERS. AN ILLUSTRATION FOR THE FEATURE ARTICLE, "IN SEARCH OF ELVIS." **MEDIUM:** WATERCOLOR, GOUACHE DECEMBER 1989

ANITA KUNZ   **ART DIRECTOR:** FRED WOODWARD   **PUBLICATION:** ROLLING STONE **PUBLISHING COMPANY:** STRAIGHT ARROW PUBLISHERS.

33

PORTRAITS OF CHUBBY CHECKER, JIMI HENDRIX, AND THE MONKEES FOR THE FEATURE, "THE HISTORY OF ROCK & ROLL." **MEDIUM:** WATERCOLOR, GOUACHE 1989

34

PUBLISHING COMPANY: WHITTLE COMMUNICATIONS. AN

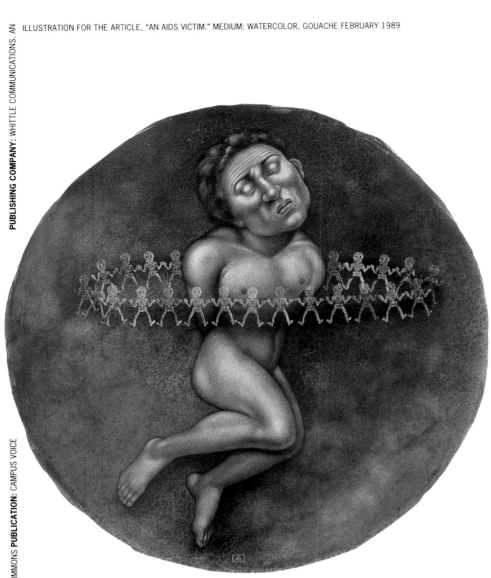

ART DIRECTOR: SU POGANY DESIGNER: JENNIFER JESSEE WRITER: CAROLE R. SIMMONS PUBLICATION: CAMPUS VOICE

ANITA KUNZ

ART DIRECTOR: MARK DANZIG **WRITER:** JANET WOOLLEY

ROBERT DAY **PUBLICATION:** THE WASHINGTON POST MAGAZINE **PUBLISHING COMPANY:** THE WASHINGTON POST.   ILLUSTRATION FOR "NOT IN KANSAS ANYMORE," A STORY ABOUT A WRITER'S RETURN TO WASHINGTON D.C. **MEDIUM:** GOUACHE OCTOBER 1989

PORTRAIT OF ANDY WARHOL FOR THE ARTICLE, "REPRO MAN." **MEDIUM:** GOUACHE, INK OCTOBER 1989

JANET WOOLLEY   **ART DIRECTOR:** PAMELA BERRY **WRITER:** EDMUND WHITE **PUBLICATION:** SAVVY **PUBLISHING COMPANY:** FAMILY MEDIA INC.

38

EVERETT PECK **ART DIRECTOR:** JOHN KORPICS **WRITER:** ANDY WARHOL (DIARIES) **PUBLICATION:** REGARDIE'S **PUBLISHING COMPANY:** REGARDIE'S, INC. FOR A FEATURE ENTITLED "WARHOL IN WASHINGTON", THE ILLUSTRATION DEPICTS THE MEDIA ASSAULT ON ANDY WARHOL ON SEPTEMBER 25TH, 1980, IN A HOTEL ROOM IN WASHINGTON D.C. **MEDIUM:** MIXED MEDIA DECEMBER 1989

ANN FIELD   **ART DIRECTOR:** JANE PALECEK **WRITER:** PATRICIA LONG **PUBLICATION:** HIPPOCRATES MAGAZINE **PUBLISHING COMPANY:** HIPPOCRATES PARTNERS INC.

JANET WOOLLEY **ART DIRECTOR:** JANE PALECEK **DESIGNER:** STEVE POWELL **WRITERS:** JOHN W. FARQUHAR, M.D. AND GENE SPILLER, PH.D. **PUBLICATION:** HIPPOCRATES MAGAZINE **PUBLISING COMPANY:** HIPPOCRATES PARTNERS INC. AN ILLUSTRATION FOR "THE LAST PUFF." THE PIECE SHOWS THE MERIT OF GIVING UP CIGARETTES.

MEDIUM: GOUACHE AND COLLAGE JANUARY/FEBRUARY 1990

DESIGNER: LISA WAGNER PUBLICATION: SAVVY PUBLISHING COMPANY: FAMILY MEDIA INC. ILLUSTRATION FOR "THE NATURAL," A PIECE ON BEAUTY. MEDIUM: PASTEL JANUARY 1990

ART DIRECTOR: BARBARA RICHER

PATTY DRYDEN

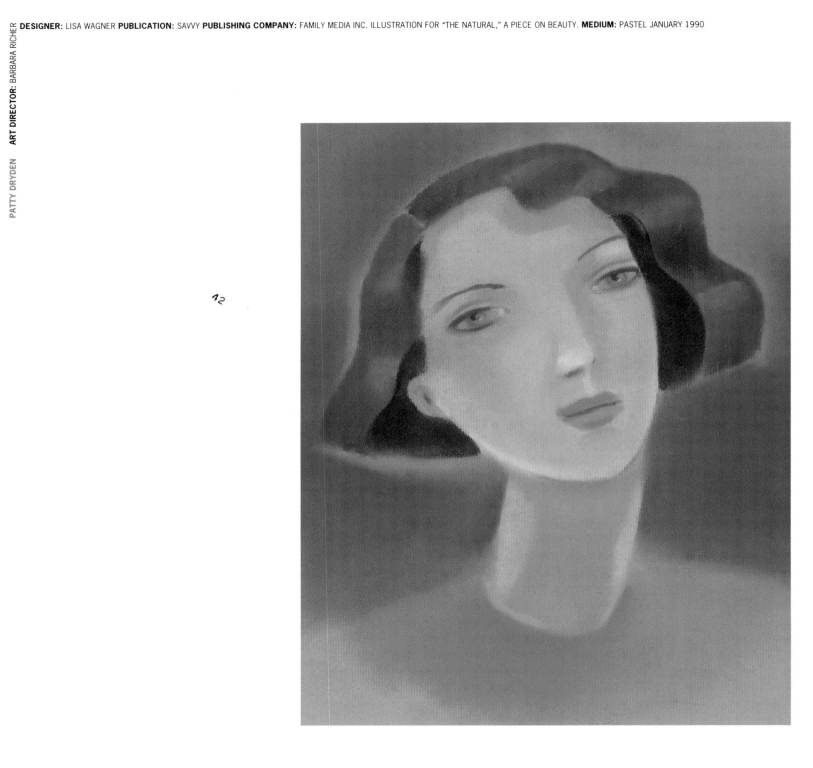

BARRY BLITT **ART DIRECTOR:** STEVE HOFFMAN **DESIGNER:** PETER HERBERT **WRITER:** E.M. SWIFT **PUBLICATION:** SPORTS ILLUSTRATED **PUBLISHING COMPANY:** TIME WARNER.

AN ILLUSTRATION FOR "OH MAGNIFICA!", A STORY ABOUT A FISHING EXPEDITION. **MEDIUM:** INK AND WATERCOLOR SEPTEMBER 1989

WRITERS: BARRY NELSON, FRANK DILEONARDI, ROBERT ELLIS **PUBLICATION:** THE WYATT COMMUNICATOR **PUBLISHING COMPANY:** THE WYATT COMPANY. ILLUSTRATION FOR "EMPLOYEE INVOLVEMENT: STRIKING THE RIGHT CHORD FOR AMERICAN BUSINESS." **MEDIUM:** CHARCOAL AND PASTELS JANUARY 1990

TROY THOMAS   **ART DIRECTOR:** AMY MCCARTER **DESIGN FIRM:** PRESSLEY JACOBS DESIGN

ANTHONY RUSSO   **ART DIRECTOR:** TERESA FERNANDES **WRITER:** NORMAN SNIDER **PUBLICATION:** TORONTO LIFE MAGAZINE **PUBLISHING COMPANY:** KEY PUBLISHERS. AN ILLUSTRATION FOR A

TRAVEL ARTICLE ON MEXICO. **MEDIUM:** ACRYLIC JANUARY 1990

ART DIRECTOR: ROBERT RISKO **PUBLICATION:** HENRY CONNELL **PUBLISHING COMPANY:** INTERVIEW ENTERPRISES, INC. PORTRAIT OF MILES DAVIS FOR INTERVIEW'S PREVIEW FEATURE. **MEDIUM:** DESIGNER'S GOUACHE SEPTEMBER 1989

JAZZ REVIEW COLUMN. **MEDIUM:** PEN & INK WITH PANTONE FILM MARCH 1990

J.D. KING   **ART DIRECTOR:** MARK MICHAELSON **WRITER:** GARY GIDDINS **PUBLICATION:** ENTERTAINMENT WEEKLY **PUBLISHING COMPANY:** TIME WARNER. ILLUSTRATION FOR A

CHARM **PUBLICATION:** LOTUS QUARTERLY **PUBLISHING COMPANY:** LOTUS DEVELOPMENT CORPORATION.   ILLUSTRATION FOR "AGENDA PROVES AN ADVANTAGE FOR THE DISADVANTAGED," AN ARTICLE ON HOW

A LOTUS DATABASE MANAGEMENT SYSTEM CAN HELP INCREASE OPPORTUNITIES FOR MINORITY VENDORS. **MEDIUM:** WATERCOLOR FALL 1989

TIM LEWIS   **ART DIRECTOR:** RONN CAMPISI **WRITER:** ROB

50

TIM LEWIS **ART DIRECTORS:** MARY WORKMAN, BETT MCLEAN **DESIGNER:** JANE HILLHOUSE **WRITER:** MARGARET READ MACDONALD

STORY ABOUT A TAILOR'S SCISSORS REVENGING HIS DEATH. **MEDIUM:** WATERCOLOR FALL 1989

PUBLICATION: STORYTELLING MAGAZINE **PUBLISHING COMPANY:** NATIONAL ASSOCIATION FOR THE PRESERVATION AND PERPETUATION OF STORYTELLING. COVER ILLUSTRATION BASED ON "THE WIZARD CLIP," A

CHARLES BURNS   **ART DIRECTOR:** FRED WOODWARD **WRITER:** DAVID FRICKE **PUBLICATION:** ROLLING STONE **PUBLISHING COMPANY:** STRAIGHT ARROW PUBLISHERS.

PHILIP BURKE **ART DIRECTOR:** FRED WOODWARD **PUBLICATION:** ROLLING STONE **PUBLISHING COMPANY:** STRAIGHT ARROW PUBLISHERS. ILLUSTRATION OF JON LOVITZ FOR TABLE OF CONTENTS PAGE. **MEDIUM:** OIL FEBRUARY 1990

STRUMMER FOR TABLE OF CONTENTS PAGE. **MEDIUM:** OIL NOVEMBER 1989

PHILIP BURKE   **ART DIRECTOR:** FRED WOODWARD **PUBLICATION:** ROLLING STONE **PUBLISHING COMPANY:** STRAIGHT ARROW PUBLISHERS.   ILLUSTRATION OF JOE

PHILIP BURKE   **ART DIRECTOR:** FRED WOODWARD **PUBLICATION:** ROLLING STONE **PUBLISHING COMPANY:** STRAIGHT ARROW PUBLISHERS.

ILLUSTRATION OF SPIKE LEE FOR TABLE OF CONTENTS PAGE. **MEDIUM:** OIL JULY 1989

53

54

PHILIP BURKE **ART DIRECTOR:** FRED WOODWARD **PUBLICATION:** ROLLING STONE **PUBLISHING COMPANY:** STRAIGHT ARROW PUBLISHERS. ILLUSTRATION OF ELVIS COSTELLO FOR TABLE OF CONTENTS PAGE. **MEDIUM:** OIL JUNE 1989

ART DIRECTOR: FRED WOODWARD **DESIGNER:** JOLENE CUYLER **PUBLICATION:** ROLLING STONE **PUBLISHING COMPANY:** STRAIGHT ARROW PUBLISHERS.   ILLUSTRATION OF MIKE TYSON FOR THE ARTICLE, "LORD OF

BRAD HOLLAND

THE RING." **MEDIUM:** ACRYLIC OCTOBER 1989

BRAD HOLLAND   **ART DIRECTOR:** JOHN KORPICS **WRITERS:** BRIAN KELLY, HARRY JAFFE **PUBLICATION:** REGARDIE'S **PUBLISHING COMPANY:** REGARDIE'S, INC.   AN ILLUSTRATION FOR AN ARTICLE ENTITLED "CONFLICTS OF INTEREST: THE FARRAKHAN FIASCO." **MEDIUM:** ACRYLIC JANUARY 1990

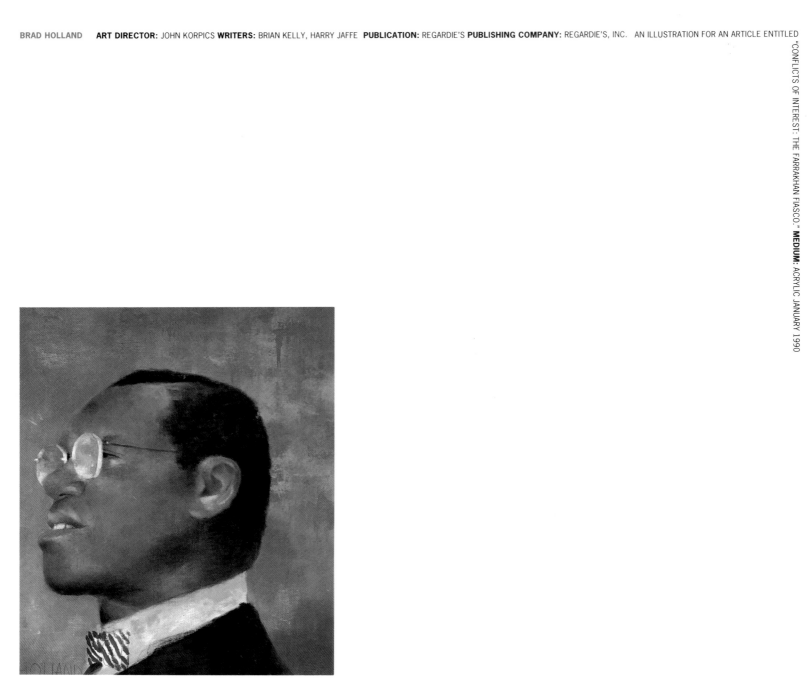

57

PUBLISHING COMPANY: PENTHOUSE. THIS PIECE IS FOR AN ARTICLE ENTITLED "HOPELESSLY DEVOTED TO YOU." MEDIUM: ACRYLIC APRIL 1990

BRAD HOLLAND   ART DIRECTORS: FRANK DEVINO, RICHARD BLEIWEISS WRITER: ROD LURIE PUBLICATION: PENTHOUSE.

MAURICE VELLEKOOP

ART DIRECTOR: GAEL TOWEY **WRITER:** JANE KRAMER **PUBLICATION:** HOUSE AND GARDEN

60

MEDIUM: PEN AND WATERCOLOR OCTOBER 1989

IN DECORATION.

PUBLISHING COMPANY: CONDE' NAST PUBLICATIONS, INC. AN ILLUSTRATION FOR "CLIMBING MT. MANHATTAN," A FEATURE ON HOW NEW YORK'S NOUVEAU RICH EMULATES THE OLD MONEY CROWD'S TASTE

BRAD HOLLAND **ART DIRECTORS:** TOM STABLER, KERIG POPE **WRITER:** NORMAN MAILER **PUBLICATION:** PLAYBOY **PUBLISHING COMPANY:** PLAYBOY ENTERPRISES INC. THIS ILLUSTRATION WAS USED FOR THE ARTICLE, "THE CHANGING OF THE THE GUARD." **MEDIUM:** ACRYLIC JANUARY 1989

PUBLISHING COMPANY: HEARST CORPORATION. AN ILLUSTRATION FOR THE ARTICLE, "WHY IS DADDY HURTING MOMMY?" MEDIUM: OIL NOVEMBER 1989

60

SANDRA HENDLER   ART DIRECTOR: RIP GEORGES DESIGNER: KATHLEEN MUNISTERI WRITER: DR. BENNET OLSHAKER PUBLICATION: ESQUIRE

JOSEPH SALINA   ART DIRECTORS: MIKE MARCUM, JIM DARILEK DESIGNER: MIKE TAYLOR WRITER: KATHLEEN MCCLEARY PUBLICATION: SPECIAL REPORT SPORTS   PUBLISHING COMPANY: WHITTLE

COMMUNICATIONS. ILLUSTRATION FOR THE ARTICLE, "THE SPACE MAN COMETH." MEDIUM: ACRYLIC NOVEMBER-JANUARY 1990

ART DIRECTOR: PETE SPINO **WRITER:** RUTHE STEIN **PUBLICATION:** THE ARIZONA DAILY STAR **PUBLISHING COMPANY:** STAR PUBLISHING CO. AN ILLUSTRATION FOR "WHAT THEY REALLY WANT..." AN ARTICLE ON MEN AND WOMEN'S MISCONCEPTIONS ABOUT SEXUAL RELATIONSHIPS. **MEDIUM:** GOUACHE AND COLORED PENCIL AUGUST 1989

PETE SPINO   **ART DIRECTOR:** PETE SPINO **PUBLICATION:** THE ARIZONA DAILY STAR **PUBLISHING COMPANY:** STAR PUBLISHING CO. AN ILLUSTRATION FOR THE FEATURE "WAR AND REMEMBRANCE." **MEDIUM:** GOUACHE AND COLORED PENCIL NOVEMBER 1989

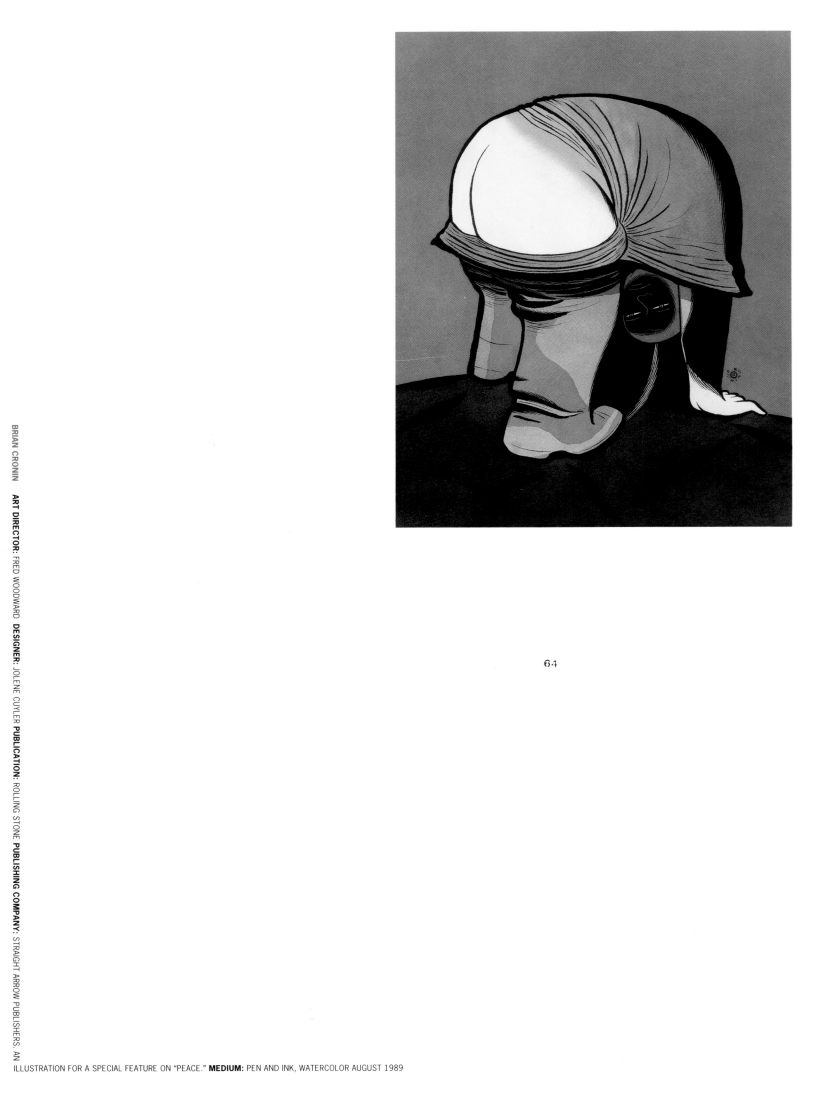

64

BRIAN CRONIN **ART DIRECTOR:** FRED WOODWARD **DESIGNER:** JOLENE CUYLER **PUBLICATION:** ROLLING STONE **PUBLISHING COMPANY:** STRAIGHT ARROW PUBLISHERS. AN

ILLUSTRATION FOR A SPECIAL FEATURE ON "PEACE." **MEDIUM:** PEN AND INK, WATERCOLOR AUGUST 1989

BRIAN CRONIN ART DIRECTOR: FRED WOODWARD DESIGNER: JOLENE CUYLER WRITER: HOWARD KOHN PUBLICATION: ROLLING STONE PUBLISHING COMPANY: STRAIGHT ARROW PUBLISHERS. ILLUSTRATION FOR THE ARTICLE, "COWBOY IN THE CAPITAL: DRUG CZAR BILL BENNETT." MEDIUM: PEN AND INK, WATERCOLOR NOVEMBER 1989

BRIAN CRONIN   **ART DIRECTOR:** PAMELA BERRY   **PUBLISHING COMPANY:** FAMILY MEDIA INC. ILLUSTRATION FOR AN   ARTICLE ENTITLED "MAKING NATURE PAY," ABOUT HOW CONSERVATIONISTS ARE SAVING WILDLIFE BY HELPING PEOPLE. **MEDIUM:** INK, GOUACHE OCTOBER 1989

WRITER: DAVID BERREBY   **PUBLICATION:** SAVVY

BRIAN CRONIN

ART DIRECTOR: PAMELA BERRY **DESIGNER:** JOHN LEE **WRITER:** GEORGE BLOOSTON **PUBLICATION:** SAVVY **PUBLISHING COMPANY:** FAMILY

68

MEDIA INC. ILLUSTRATION FOR "A CHANGE OF HEART," AN ARTICLE ON HOW WORKERS WANT GREATER REWARDS THAN MONEY. **MEDIUM:** INK, WATERCOLOR

MAGAZINE **PUBLISHING COMPANY:** HIPPOCRATES PARTNERS INC. THIS PIECE IS FOR "KICK ME, I SMOKE," AN ARTICLE BY A SMOKER WHO FEELS DISCRIMINATED AGAINST. **MEDIUM:** MIXED MEDIA JULY/AUGUST

1989

ART DIRECTOR: JANE PALECEK **WRITER:** PATRICK COOKE **PUBLICATION:** HIPPOCRATES

HENRIK DRESCHER

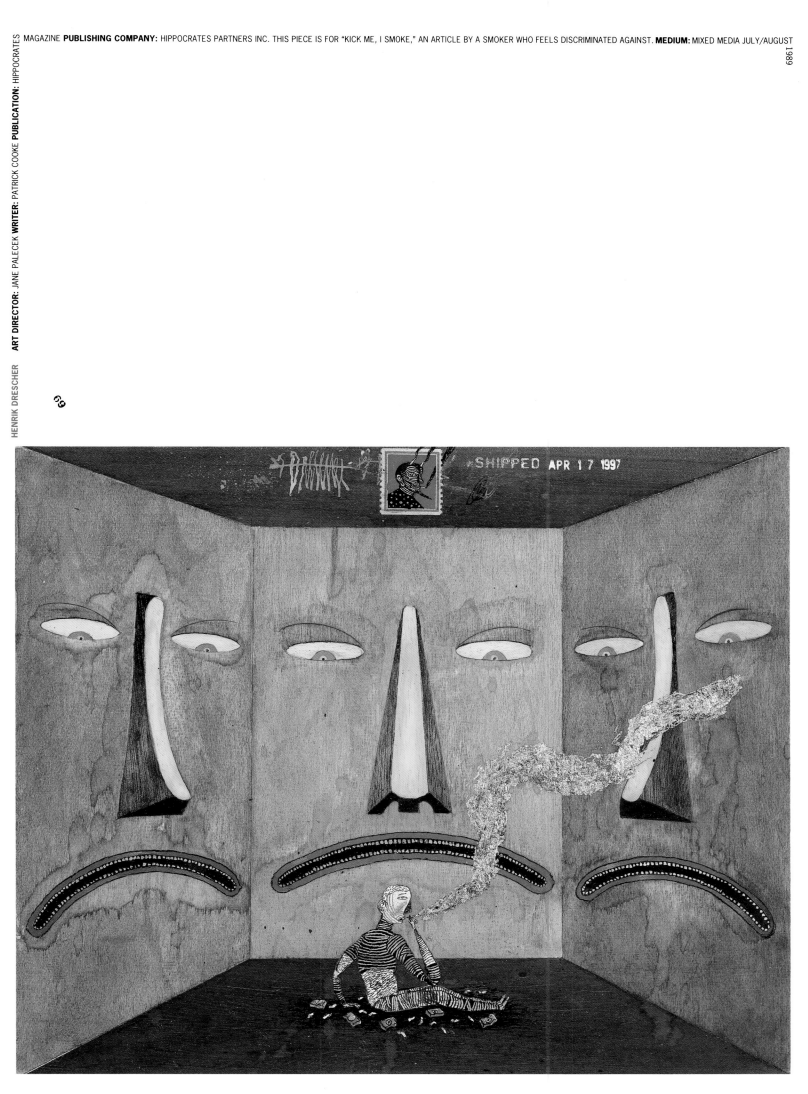

TRACY WALKER **ART DIRECTOR:** LISA J. MOORE **WRITER:** MARI LYNN LARKIN **PUBLICATION:** WEIGHT WATCHERS MAGAZINE **PUBLISHING COMPANY:** WEIGHT WATCHERS

TWENTYFIRST CORP. AN ILLUSTRATION FOR THE ARTICLE, "NUTRIENT THIEVES." **MEDIUM:** INK AND COLORED PENCIL APRIL 1990

PAUL DAVIS   ART DIRECTOR: PAUL DAVIS PUBLICATION:

WIGWAG PUBLISHING COMPANY: WIGWAG MAGAZINE COMPANY INC. AN ILLUSTRATION FOR THE COVER OF THE PREMIERE ISSUE OF WIGWAG MAGAZINE. MEDIUM: ACRYLIC ON CANVAS OCTOBER 1989

AN ILLUSTRATION FOR THE ARTICLE, "ETHICS WHERE THERE ARE NONE—A HOLOCAUST SURVIVOR REMEMBERS." **MEDIUM:** LINOLEUM CUT, COLOR PENCIL, COLLAGE JANUARY 1989

NYU MEDICAL CENTER. **PUBLISHING COMPANY:** NYU PHYSICIAN **PUBLICATION:** ALBERT HAAS, M.D. **WRITER:** VIRGINIA ATKINSON **ART DIRECTOR:** FRANCES JETTER

72

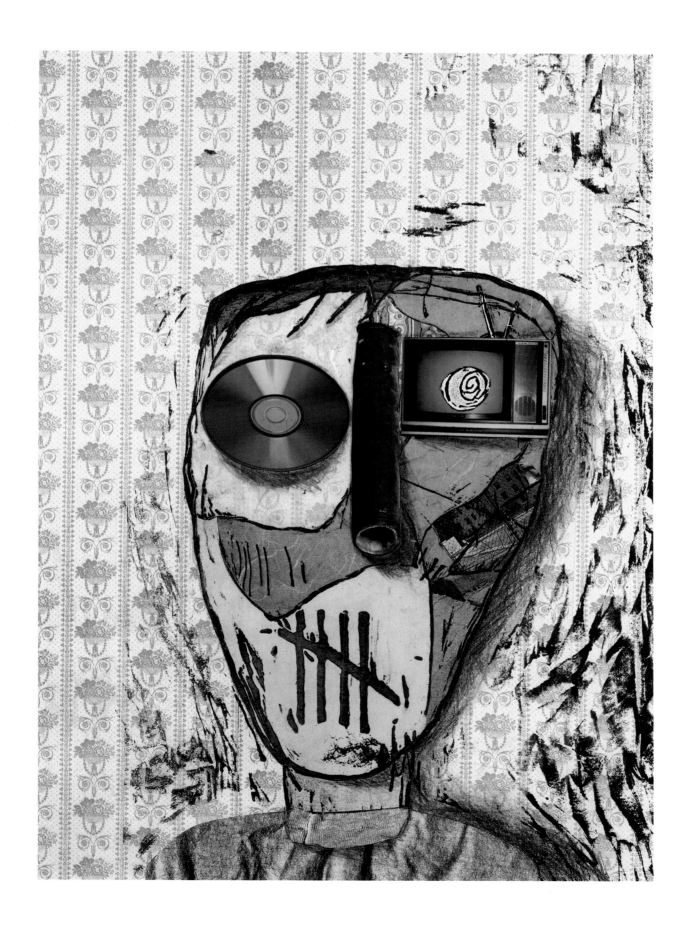

FRANCIS JETTER **ART DIRECTOR:** ARTHUR HOCHSTEIN **PUBLICATION:** TIME MAGAZINE **PUBLISHING COMPANY:** TIME WARNER. COVER ILLUSTRATION ON THE SUBJECT OF YOUTH AND VIOLENCE. **MEDIUM:** LINOLEUM CUT AND COLLAGE JUNE 1989

FRANCES JETTER **ART DIRECTOR:** NAOMI KNECHT **WRITER:** PAUL FUSSELL **PUBLICATION:** THE PENNSYLVANIA GAZETTE **PUBLISHING COMPANY:** THE UNIVERSITY OF PENNSYLVANIA'S GENERAL ALUMNI SOCIETY. AN ILLUSTRATION FOR THE ARTICLE "FEAR AND BLUNDERING IN WORLD WAR II." **MEDIUM:** LINOLEUM CUT, XEROXES, METAL, COLLAGE OCTOBER 1989

C.F. PAYNE **ART DIRECTOR:** FRED WOODWARD **PUBLICATION:** ROLLING STONE **PUBLISHING COMPANY:** STRAIGHT ARROW PUBLISHERS. PORTRAIT OF RICHARD NIXON AS STEVE MARTIN FOR THE ARTICLE, "WELL PARDON ME." **MEDIUM:** MIXED

MEDIA NOVEMBER 1989

A COLLAGE FOR "JAPAN BUYS A USED PRESIDENT", AN ARTICLE ON RONALD REAGAN'S COMMERCIAL ADVENTURES AFTER HE LEFT THE OVAL OFFICE. **MEDIUM:** COLLAGE NOVEMBER 1989

STEPHEN KRONINGER   **ART DIRECTOR:** MICHAEL VALENTE   **WRITER:** LARRY GELBART   **PUBLICATION:** THE NEW YORK TIMES **PUBLISHING COMPANY:** THE NEW YORK TIMES CO.

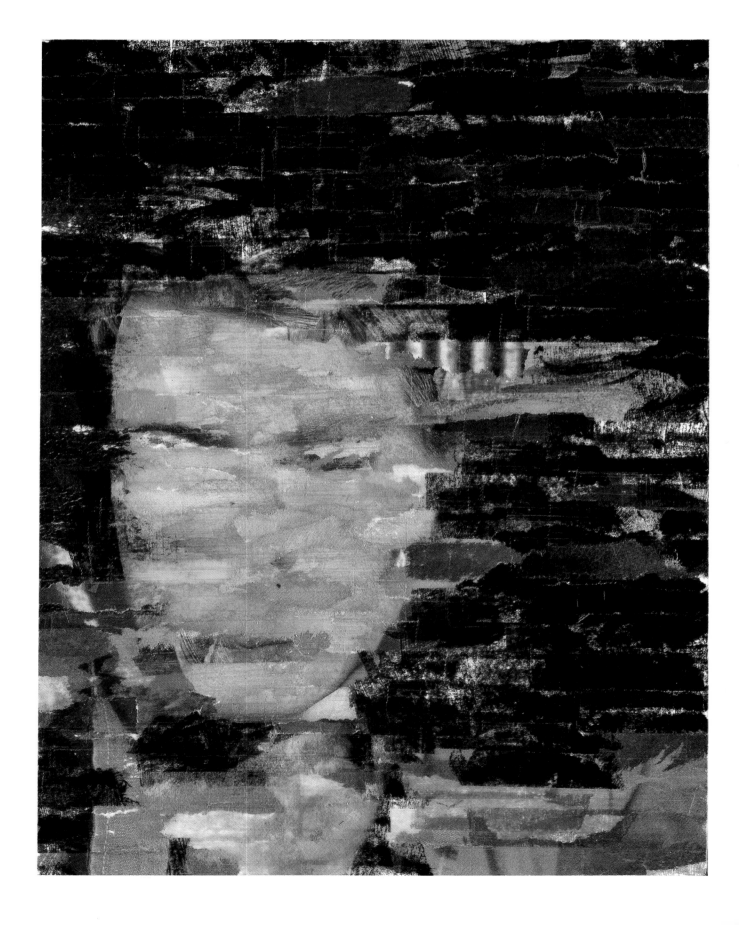

STEPHEN KRONINGER   **ART DIRECTOR:** JOHN HOUSTON **PUBLICATION:** NEWSWEEK, INC. AN ILLUSTRATION FOR AN ARTICLE ENTITLED, "WHY MEN RAPE." **MEDIUM:** COLLAGE JUNE 1989

STEPHEN KRONINGER   **ART DIRECTOR:** MICHAEL VALENTE **WRITER:** LEWIS GROSSBERGER **PUBLICATION:** THE NEW YORK TIMES **PUBLISHING COMPANY:** THE NEW YORK TIMES CO. AN ILLUSTRATION FOR AN ARTICLE ENTITLED "THE BIG TWO TRIPLE O, LET'S PARTY." **MEDIUM:** COLLAGE AUGUST 1989

COMPANY: HIPPOCRATES PARTNERS INC. THIS ILLUSTRATION IS FOR "RADON CALLING," AN ARTICLE ON HUSTLERS SCAMMING PEOPLE OVER THE RADON GAS SCARE. **MEDIUM:** WATERCOLOR, PEN AND INK

ALAN COBER   **ART DIRECTOR:** JANE PALECEK **WRITER:** ANTHONY SCHMITZ **PUBLICATION:** HIPPOCRATES MAGAZINE **PUBLISHING**

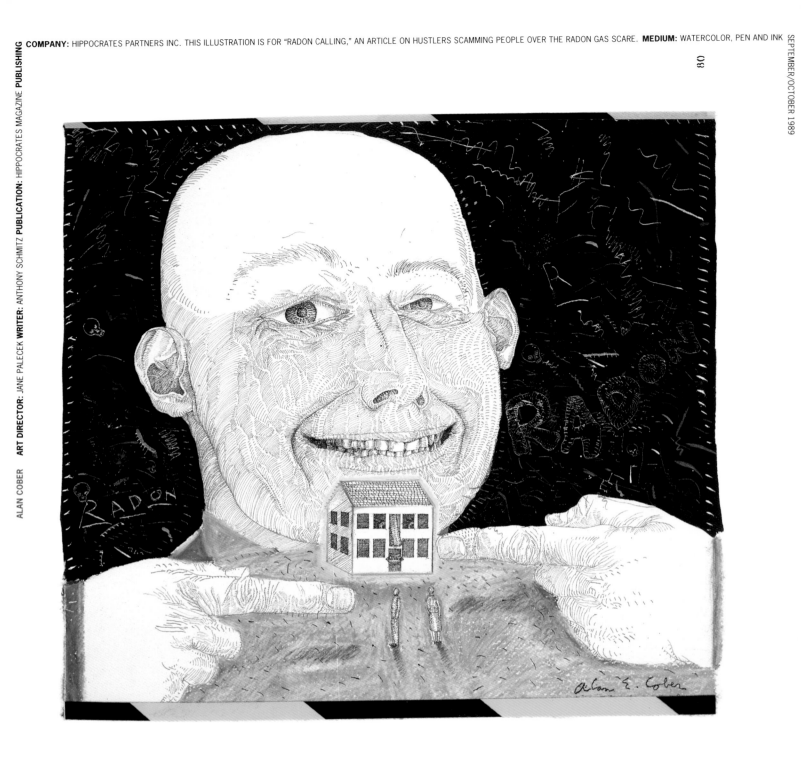

PETER KUPER   **ART DIRECTOR:** HOLLY NIXHOLM   **WRITER:** WILLIAM A. DAVIS   **PUBLICATION:** THE BOSTON GLOBE   **PUBLISHING COMPANY:** AFFILIATED PUBLICATIONS.

THIS ILLUSTRATION WAS USED FOR AN ARTICLE ON EUROPEAN TRAVEL IN THE 1990'S. **MEDIUM:** KRYLON PAINT, WATERCOLORS, COLORED PENCILS, AND COLLAGE JANUARY 1990

PETER KUPER **ART DIRECTOR:** PETER KUPER **PUBLISHING COMPANY:** INX PUBLISHING COMPANY: UNITED FEATURES SYNDICATE. AN ILLUSTRATION FOR "FEAR OF FLYING." **MEDIUM:** STENCIL SPRAYED WITH ENAMEL PAINT JANUARY 1990

EVERETT PECK **ART DIRECTOR:** KERRY TREMAIN **WRITER:** MOLLY IVINE **PUBLICATION:** MOTHER JONES MAGAZINE **PUBLISHING COMPANY:** THE FOUNDATION FOR NATIONAL PROGRESS. PORTRAIT OF VICE PRESIDENT DAN QUAYLE, FOR AN ARTICLE ENTITLED "FROM CIA TO KGB", (A KINDER GENTLER BUSH). FOR THIS STORY, SEVERAL ILLUSTRATORS WERE ASKED TO

COMMENT ON THE NEW BUSH ADMINISTRATION. **MEDIUM:** GOUACHE APRIL 1989

ILLUSTRATION FOR "THE GREAT PRETENDER," A STORY ABOUT A CON MAN. **MEDIUM:** OIL. MARCH 1990

87

MARTINE LIEBERMAN   **ART DIRECTOR:** DAVID CARSON **PUBLICATION:** BEACH CULTURE MAGAZINE **PUBLISHING COMPANY:** SURFER PUBLICATIONS. ILLUSTRATION FOR A START-UP PUBLICATION FOCUSED ON THE CALIFORNIA LIFESTYLE. **MEDIUM:** LINOLEUM CUT, COLLAGE SPRING 1990

JAMIE BENNETT **ART DIRECTOR:** JENNIFER NAPIER **DESIGNER:** BILL GRIMES **WRITER:** OMAR S. CASTANEDA **PUBLICATION:** SPECIAL REPORT (ON FICTION) **PUBLISHING COMPANY:** WHITTLE COMMUNICATIONS. ILLUSTRATION

FOR FICTION, "UNDER A BLINDING SUN." **MEDIUM:** DYES AUGUST–OCTOBER 1989

SOMMER **PUBLICATION:** ART DIRECTION MAGAZINE **PUBLISHING COMPANY** ADVERTISING TRADE PUBLICATIONS, INC. COVER ILLUSTRATION FOR ANIMATION ISSUE. **MEDIUM:** PEN & INK, WATERCOLOR APRIL 1989

PATRICK MCDONNELL **ART DIRECTOR:** SHOSHANNA

J. OTTO SEIBOLD ART DIRECTOR: GORDON SMITH PUBLICATION: CALIFORNIA LAWYER. AN ILLUSTRATION FOR AN ARTICLE ENTITLED "HOTEL CITY 1990." MEDIUM: COMPUTER APRIL 1990

ZAITSCHEK **PUBLICATION:** WIGWAG MAGAZINE **PUBLISHING COMPANY:** WIGWAG MAGAZINE CO. INC. AN ILLUSTRATION DEPICTING PROM NIGHT IN AMERICA, FOR THE COVER OF WIGWAG. **MEDIUM:** COMPUTER MAY 1990

J. OTTO SEIBOLD   **ART DIRECTOR:** PAUL DAVIS **DESIGNER:** RISA

AN ILLUSTRATION FOR THE ESSAY, "IN THE FOOTSTEPS OF A MARATHON VETERAN." **MEDIUM:** PENCILS, OVERLAYS NOVEMBER 1989

MICHAEL S. KLEIN   **ART DIRECTOR:** FRED NORGAARD **WRITER:** MARC BLOOM **PUBLICATION:** THE NEW YORK TIMES **PUBLISHING COMPANY:** THE NEW YORK TIMES CO.

THE NEW YORK TIMES MAGAZINE **PUBLISHING COMPANY:** THE NEW YORK TIMES CO. ILLUSTRATION FOR THE ARTICLE, "WHERE EAST MEETS WEST—TO BOOGIE!" **MEDIUM:** LINOLEUM BLOCK PRINT, COLOR

OVERLAYS MARCH 1990

MICHAEL BARTALOS **PUBLICATION:** **ART DIRECTOR:** RICHARD WEIGAND **WRITER:** WILLIAM H. GASS

ANTHONY RUSSO   **ART DIRECTOR:** MARILYN BABCOCK   **DESIGNER:** JODI NAKATSUKA   **PUBLICATION:** L.A. STYLE MAGAZINE   **PUBLISHING COMPANY:** AMERICAN EXPRESS

PUBLISHING CORP., AUGUST 1989.   THIS ILLUSTRATION WAS FEATURED WITH THE ARTICLE "NO FREE LUNCH–CONFESSIONS OF A FOOD CRITIC."   **MEDIUM:** SCRATCHBOARD.

AN ILLUSTRATION FOR A QUESTIONNAIRE ENTITLED, "WHAT ARE YOUR VALUES AND GOALS?" **MEDIUM:** GOUACHE MAY 1989

SANDRA DIONISI   **ART DIRECTOR:** FO WILSON **DESIGNER:** JENNIFER B. GILLMAN **PUBLICATION:** PSYCHOLOGY TODAY **PUBLISHING COMPANY:** P.T. PARTNERS.

SANDRA DIONISI   **ART DIRECTOR:** BRUCE WRIGHT **WRITER:** ROBERT COATES **PUBLICATION:** CANADIAN LAWYER **PUBLICATION COMPANY:** CANADA LAW BOOK, INC. THIS PIECE IS FOR "PRIVATE EYES," AN ARTICLE ON THE INCREASINGLY COMMON PRACTICE OF USING PRIVATE INVESTIGATORS TO ASSIST LAWYERS IN THE COLLECTION OF EVIDENCE. **MEDIUM:** GOUACHE MAY 1989

102

BLAIR DRAWSON **DESIGNER:** DAVID ARMARIO **WRITER:** SUSAN FALUDI **PUBLICATION:** WEST MAGAZINE **PUBLISHING COMPANY:** SAN JOSE MERCURY NEWS. THIS ILLUSTRATION OF A BARREN WOMAN WAS USED FOR AN ARTICLE ON CAREER WOMEN WHO ARE SUFFERING FROM THE EMPTY WOMB SYNDROME. **MEDIUM:** WATERCOLOR AND COLOR PENCILS APRIL 1989

LILLA ROGERS **ART DIRECTOR:** RICHARD FERRETTI **WRITER:** ELLEN STERN **PUBLICATION:** CHILD MAGAZINE **PUBLISHING COMPANY:** THE NEW YORK

"MOTHER'S DAY WISH LIST." **MEDIUM:** OIL FEBRUARY 1990

TIMES CO. ILLUSTRATION OF THE ARTICLE,

ARTICLE ON NEW KOSHER WINES. **MEDIUM:** PASTEL, GOUACHE, MARBLEIZED PAPER APRIL 1989

FOR MURDER," AN ARTICLE ABOUT A MEETING WHERE PLANS WERE MADE FOR THE EXTERMINATION OF JEWS. **MEDIUM:** PASTEL, WATERCOLOR, GOUACHE MAY 1989

LILLA ROGERS   **ART DIRECTOR:** LARRY CLOSS   **WRITER:** DESMOND RYAN **PUBLICATION:** APPLAUSE MAGAZINE   **PUBLISHING COMPANY:** WHYY. THIS PIECE IS FOR "AN AGENDA

LILLA ROGERS   **ART DIRECTOR:** PATRICK MITCHELL   **DESIGNER:** HANS TEENSMA   **PUBLICATION:** MUSICIAN MAGAZINE   **PUBLISHING COMPANY:** BILLBOARD PUBLICATIONS, INC.   PORTRAIT OF TRACY CHAPMAN AND BOB DYLAN FOR AN ARTICLE ENTITLED "LIVING IN A POLITICAL WORLD—

DYLAN & CHAPMAN TAKE THE HIGHER GROUND."   **MEDIUM:** PASTEL, GOUACHE, WATERCOLOR OCTOBER 1989

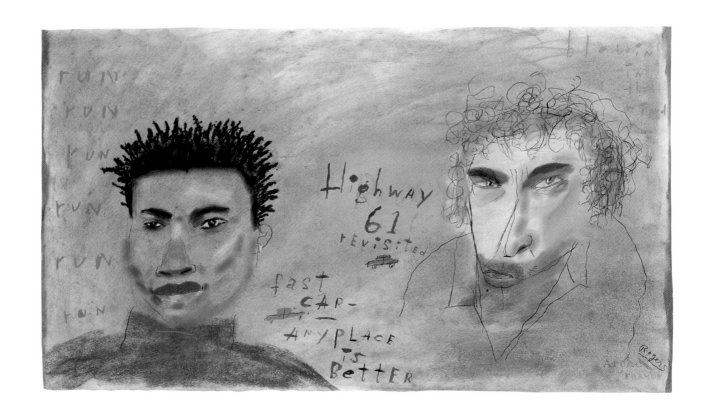

JACOBS **PUBLICATION:** THE ATLANTIC MONTHLY **PUBLISHING COMPANY:** THE ATLANTIC MONTHLY CO. ILLUSTRATION FOR THE SHORT STORY, "STONE COWBOY ON THE HIGH PLAINS." **MEDIUM:** OIL PASTEL. JUNE 1989

DENISE CHAPMAN CRAWFORD   **ART DIRECTOR:** JUDY GARLAN **WRITER:** MARK

DOLORES FAIRMAN   **ART DIRECTOR:** CATHERINE CALDWELL **DESIGNER:** TRISH MCGINITY

WRITER: JOYCE MAYNARD **PUBLICATION:** NEW WOMAN **PUBLISHING COMPANY:** MURDOCH MAGAZINES. ILLUSTRATION FOR THE SHORT STORY, "ENCOUNTER WITH A STRANGER." **MEDIUM:** GOUACHE AND COLORED PENCIL OCTOBER 1989

MAURICE VELLEKOOP **ART DIRECTOR:** DEB HARDISON **DESIGNER:** RICHARD BATES **WRITER:** GARY GIDDENS

PUBLICATION: PURSUITS **PUBLISHING COMPANY:** WHITTLE COMMUNICATIONS. ILLUSTRATIONS FOR "ONCE IN A BLUE MOOD," A FEATURE ON THE ALLURE OF JAZZ MUSIC. **MEDIUM:** WATERCOLOR SUMMER 1989

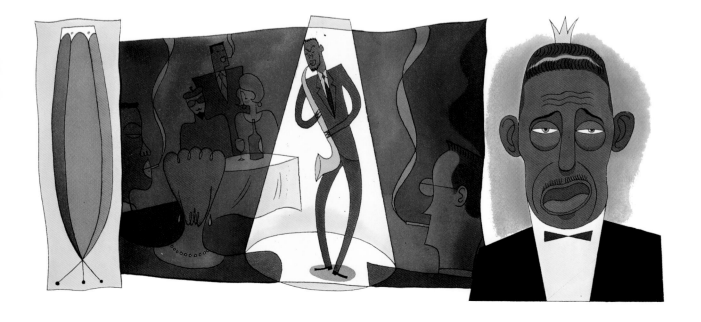

113

PUBLISHING COMPANY: VISTA PUBLICATIONS. AN ILLUSTRATION FOR "THE MORNING AFTER," AN ARTICLE CONTEMPLATING THE RESULTS IF QUEBEC BREAKS AWAY FROM CANADA AND BECOMES A SEPARATE COUNTRY. MEDIUM: ACRYLIC MARCH 1990

VALERIE SINCLAIR ART DIRECTOR: ROD DELLA VEDOVA WRITER: JAN MATTHEWS PUBLICATION: VISTA MAGAZINE

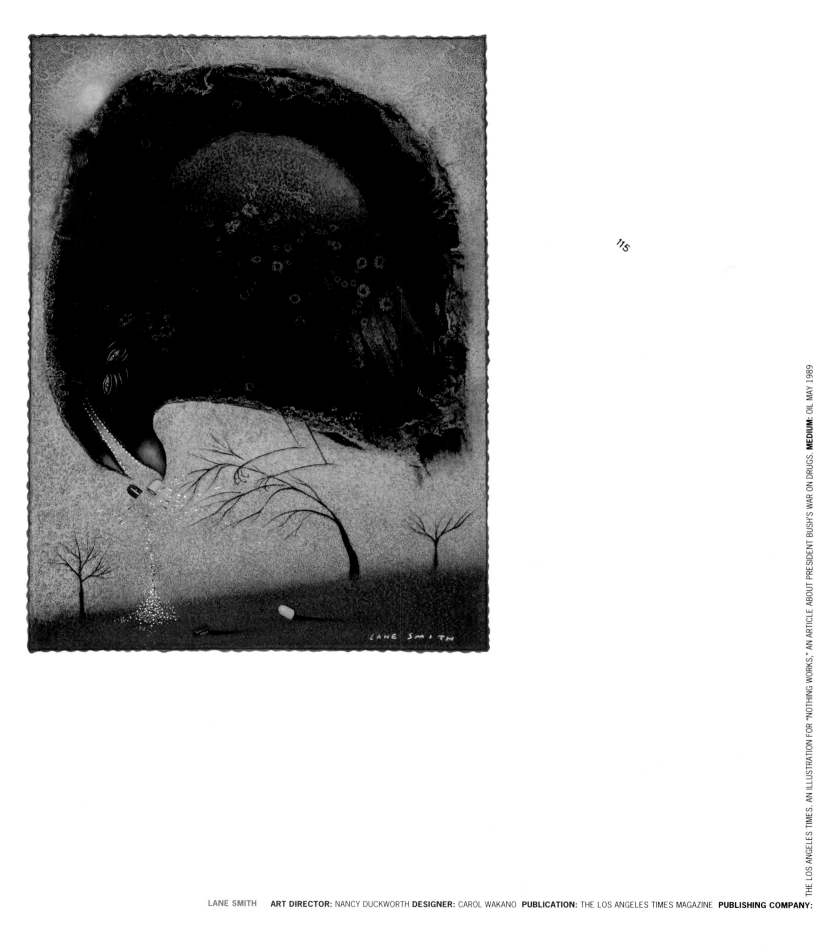

THE LOS ANGELES TIMES. AN ILLUSTRATION FOR "NOTHING WORKS," AN ARTICLE ABOUT PRESIDENT BUSH'S WAR ON DRUGS. **MEDIUM:** OIL MAY 1989

LANE SMITH   **ART DIRECTOR:** NANCY DUCKWORTH **DESIGNER:** CAROL WAKANO **PUBLICATION:** THE LOS ANGELES TIMES MAGAZINE **PUBLISHING COMPANY:**

THIS ILLUSTRATION IS FOR AN ARTICLE ON PSYCHOACOUSTICS, ENTITLED "PSYCHO-WHAT?" **MEDIUM:** OIL AND COLLAGE SEPTEMBER 1989

LANE SMITH   **ART DIRECTOR:** SUE LLEWELLYN **WRITER:** KEN C. POHLMANN   **PUBLICATION:** STEREO REVIEW **PUBLISHING COMPANY:** DIAMANDIS COMMUNICATIONS INC.

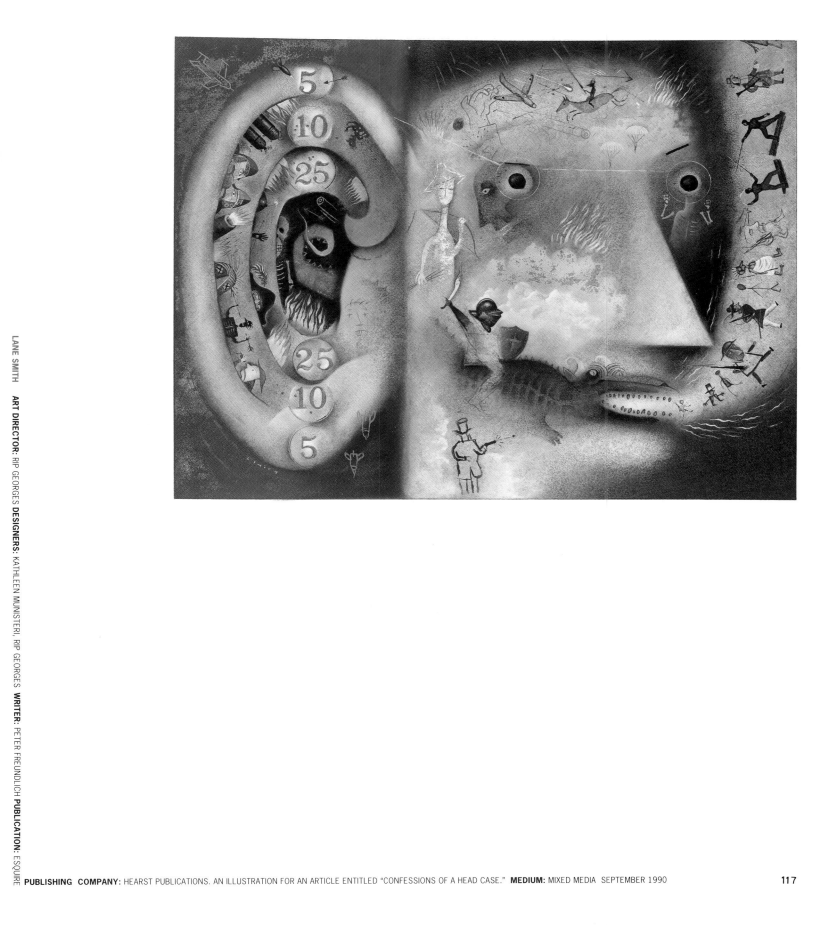

LANE SMITH **ART DIRECTOR:** RIP GEORGES **DESIGNERS:** KATHLEEN MUNISTERI, RIP GEORGES **WRITER:** PETER FREUNDLICH **PUBLICATION:** ESQUIRE

PUBLISHING COMPANY: HEARST PUBLICATIONS. AN ILLUSTRATION FOR AN ARTICLE ENTITLED "CONFESSIONS OF A HEAD CASE." **MEDIUM:** MIXED MEDIA SEPTEMBER 1990

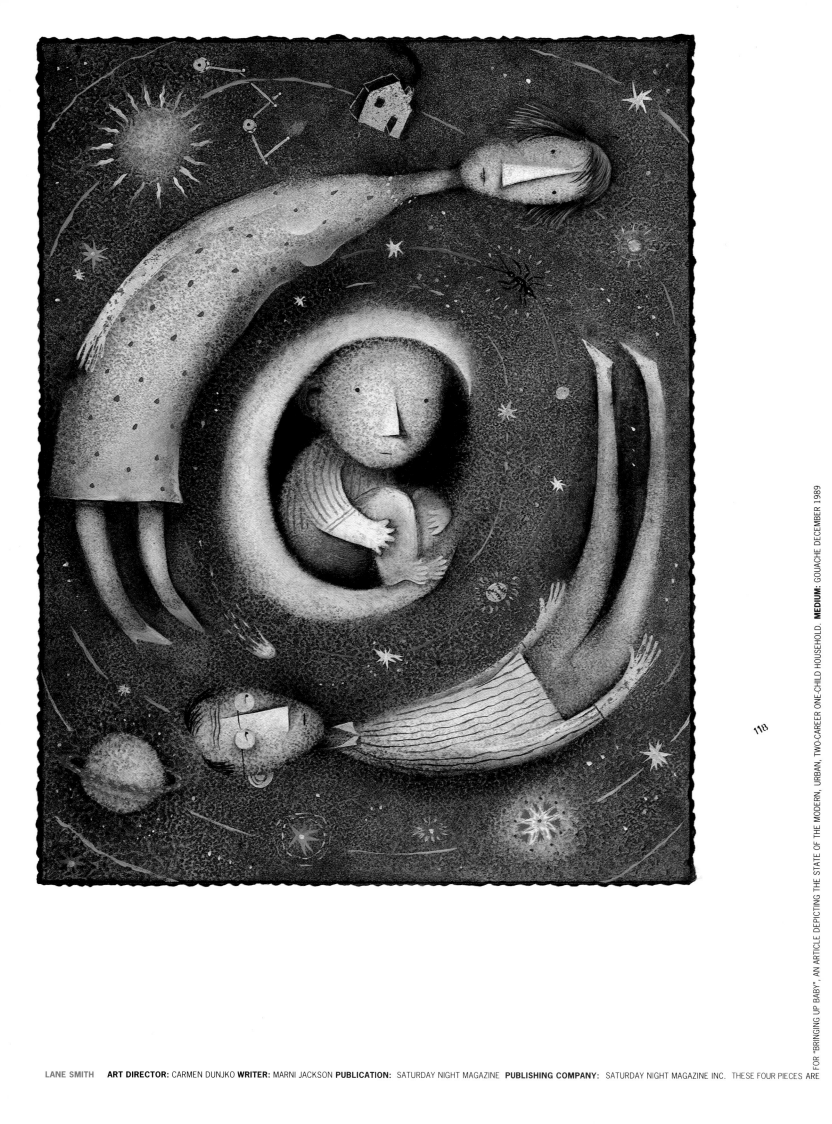

FOR "BRINGING UP BABY", AN ARTICLE DEPICTING THE STATE OF THE MODERN, URBAN, TWO-CAREER ONE-CHILD HOUSEHOLD. **MEDIUM:** GOUACHE DECEMBER 1989

LANE SMITH   **ART DIRECTOR:** CARMEN DUNJKO **WRITER:** MARNI JACKSON **PUBLICATION:** SATURDAY NIGHT MAGAZINE **PUBLISHING COMPANY:** SATURDAY NIGHT MAGAZINE INC. THESE FOUR PIECES ARE

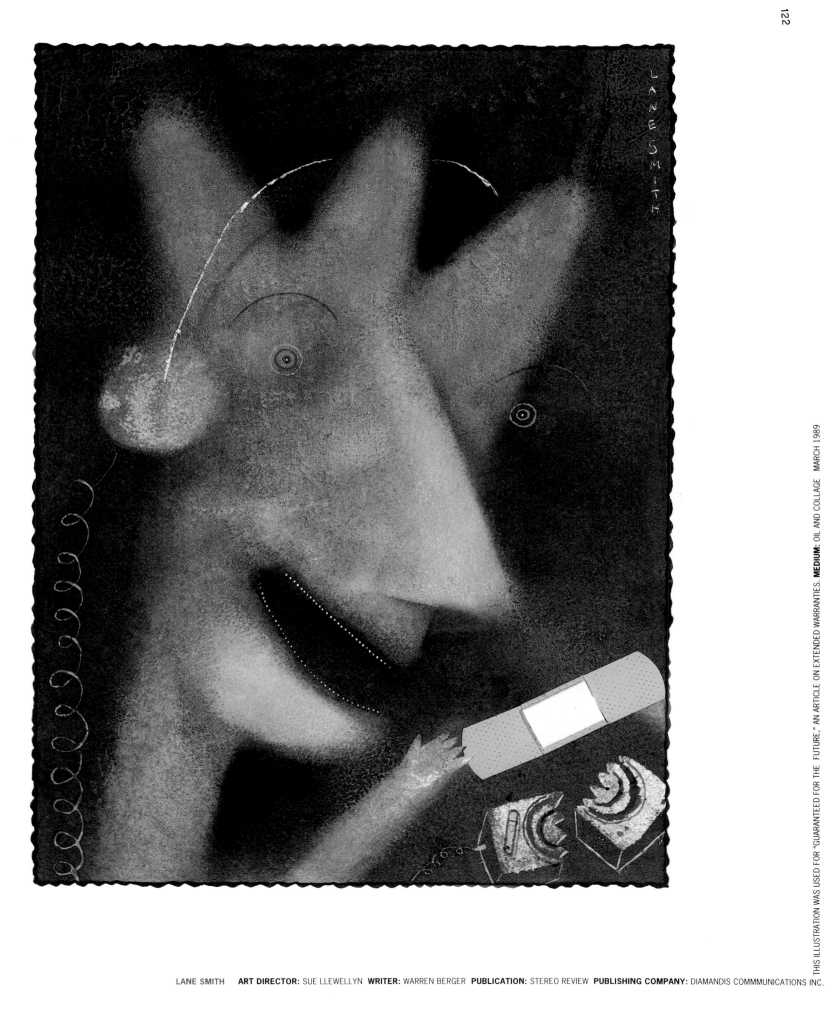

THIS ILLUSTRATION WAS USED FOR "GUARANTEED FOR THE FUTURE," AN ARTICLE ON EXTENDED WARRANTIES. **MEDIUM:** OIL AND COLLAGE MARCH 1989

LANE SMITH **ART DIRECTOR:** SUE LLEWELLYN **WRITER:** WARREN BERGER **PUBLICATION:** STEREO REVIEW **PUBLISHING COMPANY:** DIAMANDIS COMMMUNICATIONS INC.

HIPPOCRATES PARTNERS INC. A PIECE FOR "SCARED TO DEATH," AN ARTICLE ON THE POSSIBILITY OF DEATH FROM FRIGHT. **MEDIUM:** OIL MARCH/APRIL 1989

LANE SMITH   ART DIRECTOR: JOHN KORPICS   PUBLICATION: REGARDIE'S   PUBLISHING COMPANY: REGARDIE'S, INC. THIS ILLUSTRATION IS FOR THE "ADVENTURES IN MONEY" PAGE. **MEDIUM:** MIXED MEDIA JANUARY 1989

LANE SMITH **ART DIRECTOR:** LUCY BARTHOLOMAY **WRITER:** DANIEL GOLDEN **PUBLICATION:** THE BOSTON GLOBE MAGAZINE **PUBLISHING COMPANY:** AFFILIATED PUBLICATIONS. AN ILLUSTRATION FOR "GIVE ME AN E, GIVE ME AN S," AN ARTICLE ON PERSONALITY TESTING. **MEDIUM:**

125

PUBLISHING COMPANY: CONDE' NAST PUBLICATIONS, INC. AN ILLUSTRATION FOR THE ARTICLE "THE DRILL IS GONE," ABOUT OVERCOMING THE FEAR OF DENTISTS. **MEDIUM:** MIXED MEDIA NOVEMBER 1989

LANE SMITH **ART DIRECTOR:** ROBERT PRIEST **DESIGNER:** CHARLENE BENSON **WRITER:** MICHAEL KAPLAN **PUBLICATION:** G.Q. MAGAZINE

LANE SMITH **ART DIRECTOR:** SUE LLEWELLYN **WRITER:** IAN G. MASTERS **PUBLICATION:** STEREO REVIEW **PUBLISHING COMPANY:** DIAMANDIS COMMUNICATIONS INC. AN ILLUSTRATION FOR "THE AUDIBILITY OF DISTORTION," AN ARTICLE ON SOUND DISTORTION. **MEDIUM:** OIL AND COLLAGE JANUARY 1989

PUBLISHING THE WASHINGTON POST MAGAZINE **PUBLICATION:** THE WASHINGTON POST MAGAZINE **WRITER:** HENRY ALLEN **ART DIRECTOR:** MARK DANZIG LANE SMITH

128

LANE SMITH **ART DIRECTOR:** FRED WOODWARD **DESIGNER:** GAIL ANDERSON **WRITER:** TERRI MINSKY **PUBLICATION:** ROLLING STONE **PUBLISHING COMPANY:** STRAIGHT

ARROW PUBLISHERS. THIS PIECE ILLUSTRATES THE COMPETITION BETWEEN TWO COMEDY CHANNELS, FOR AN ARTICLE ENTITLED "THE 8000- HOUR JOKE." **MEDIUM:** MIXED MEDIA NOVEMBER 1989

MILTON GLASER **ART DIRECTORS:** MILTON GLASER, WALTER BERNARD, SHELLEY FISHER **PUBLISHER:**LYNNE SCANLON **PUBLISHING COMPANY:** A/ S/ M COMMUNICATIONS, INC. **TITLE:** THE ADWEEK PORTFOLIO OF ILLUSTRATION. COVER FOR ADWEEK PORTFOLIO, A DIRECTORY OF ILLUSTRATORS. **MEDIUM:** WATERCOLOR

DESIGNERS: WALTER BERNARD,

ELWOOD SMITH

LANE SMITH ART DIRECTOR: BARBARA HENNESY AUTHOR: JON SCIESZKA EDITOR: REGINA HAYES PUBLISHER: VIKING KESTREL TITLE: THE TRUE STORY OF THE 3 LITTLE PIGS. A HUMOROUS RETELLING OF THE 3 LITTLE PIGS FROM THE WOLF'S POINT OF VIEW. MEDIUM: OIL.

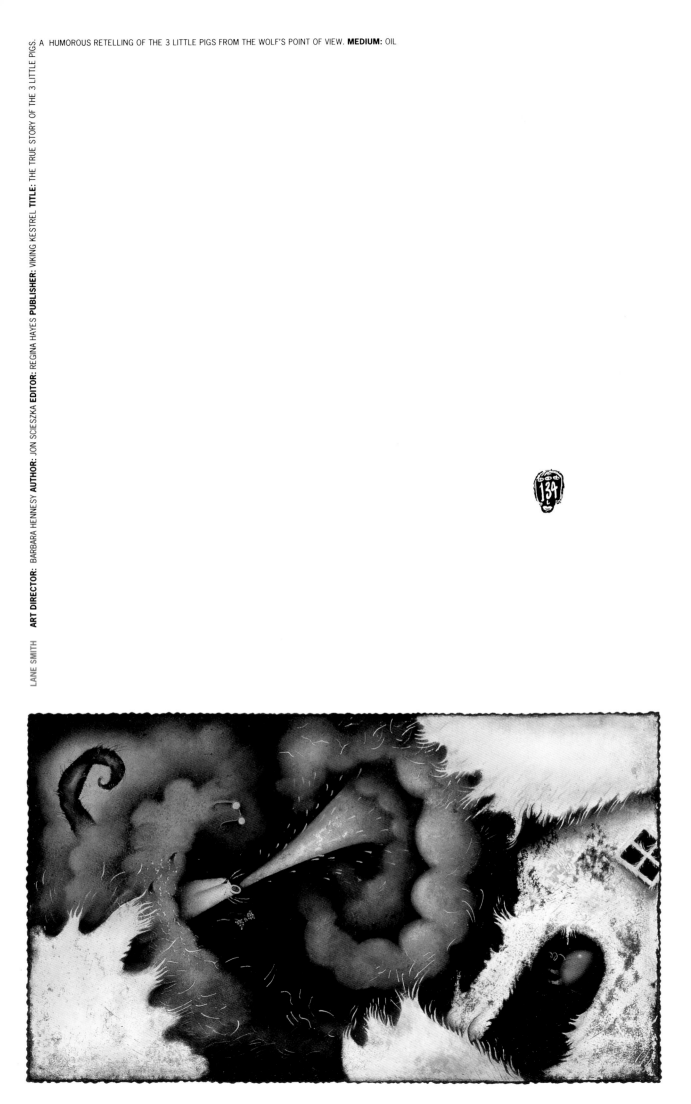

EDITOR: JOHN WINDLE **PUBLISHER:** DAILEY RARE BOOKS **PUBLISHING CO.:** W & V DAILEY, LTD. **TITLE:** CATALOGUE 56—ENGLISH LITERATURE. BENNETT CREATED THIS GRAPHIC PIECE WITH GEOMETRIC SHAPES,

TYPE, AND DAILEY'S SIGNATURE HORN-RIMMED GLASSES. **MEDIUM:** INK, COLLAGE

DESIGNER: DIANNE BENNETT **AUTHOR:** WILLIAM DAILEY

DIANNE BENNETT

¶ Third Edition. Of the first edition of 1869 only a few copies are know... ...4 sec-...d edition is very ra... rare. ...re was ...m in ...video in 18... ...ving in ...ght in ...67 ... Paris an... ...n of ... in various... ...t his own... compo... ...Ducasse die... this bo... publi... this posthumous... ...red ...e received wide recognition, particu-...rly through Huysmans and Rémy de Gourmont. But it was the Surrealists who

JAVIER ROMERO **DESIGNER:** SUSAN MITCHELL **AUTHOR:** JAMES WELDON JOHNSON

MEDIUM: GOUACHE AND AIRBRUSH

OF A WHITE MAN.

EDITOR: LUANN WALTHER **PUBLISHER:** VINTAGE **PUBLISHING CO.:** RANDOM HOUSE **TITLE:** THE AUTOBIOGRAPHY OF AN EX-COLOURED MAN. THIS NOVEL IS ABOUT A FAIR-SKINNED BLACK MAN LIVING THE LIFE

MERRITT DEKLE   **DESIGNER:** NEIL STUART   **AUTHOR:** MICKEY FRIEDMAN **PUBLISHER:** VIKING · PENGUIN **TITLE:** A TEMPORARY GHOST. THIS BOOK IS ABOUT A WRITER WHO

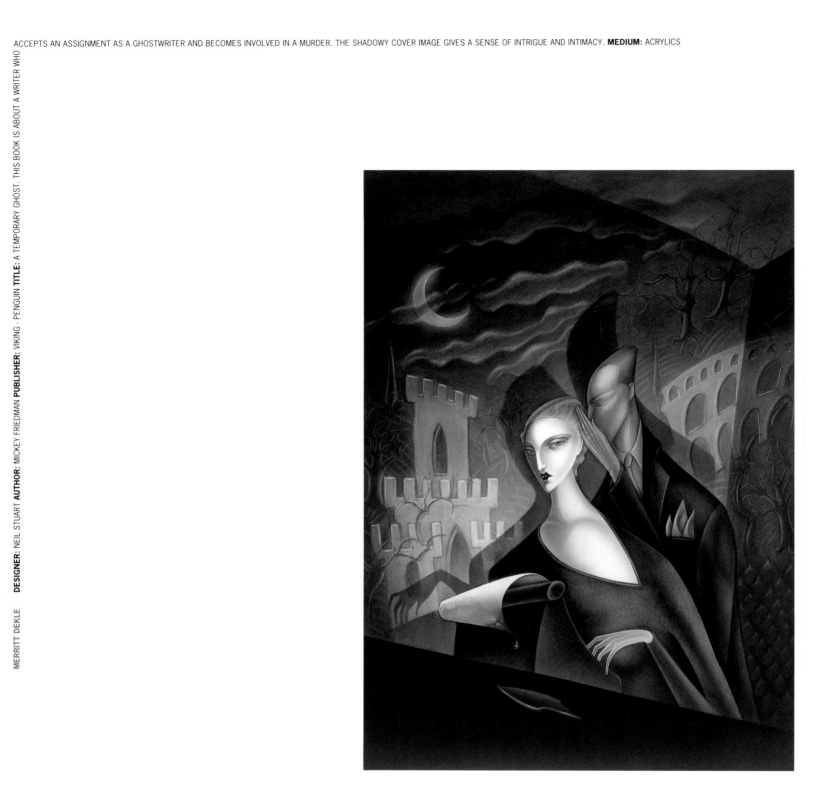

SCOTT W. HUNT **ART DIRECTOR:** MARTHA PHILLIPS **AUTHOR:** VERA CASPARY **EDITOR:** LYDIA DRISCOLL

PASTEL AND CHARCOAL

PUBLISHER: THE FRANKLIN LIBRARY **TITLE:** LAURA. HUNT WAS ASKED TO CREATE AN IMAGE OF A BEAUTIFUL WOMAN WITH A SENSE OF DANGER, MYSTERY, AND ELEGANCE FOR THIS MYSTERY NOVEL. **MEDIUM:**

ANTHONY RUSSO **DESIGNER:** SARA EISENMAN **AUTHOR:** CRAIG LESLEY

PUBLISHER: HOUGHTON MIFFLIN **TITLE:** RIVERSONG. RUSSO'S ILLUSTRATION DEPICTS INDIAN GHOSTS HAUNTING A RIVER. **MEDIUM:** SCRATCHBOARD

AUTHOR: GUNTER GRASS EDITOR: ERROLL MCDONALD PUBLISHER: VINTAGE PUBLISHING CO.: RANDOM HOUSE TITLE: THE TIN DRUM. A HORRIFIC IMAGE OF THE STUNTED DRUMMER BOY FROM THE FAMOUS GERMAN NOVEL, THE TIN DRUM.

ANGELA ARNET   DESIGNER: MARC COHEN ART DIRECTOR: SUSAN MITCHELL

ART DIRECTOR: WENDY BASS **AUTHOR:** RICHARD POWERS **PUBLISHER:** COLLIER BOOKS **PUBLISHING CO.:** MACMILLIAN PUBLISHING CO. **TITLE:** PRISONERS DILEMMA. THIS ILLUSTRATION DEPICTS A MAN LOSING HIS MIND TO A FANTASY. **MEDIUM:** COLLAGE, PANTONE OVERLAYS

ROBERT CLYDE ANDERSON **ART DIRECTOR:** ALBERT CROCHET **AUTHOR:** MADISON JONES **EDITOR:** BARBARA PHILLIPS **PUBLISHER:** LOUISIANA STATE UNIVERSITY **TITLE:** LAST

JAMES DEACON   **ART DIRECTOR:** TYLER SMITH **WRITER:** GEOFF CURRIER **CLIENT:** ELITE COLOR GROUP **PUBLICATION:** AD/COM; SEPTEMBER 1989. THIS ILLUSTRATION WAS USED IN THE "ART POLICE" CAMPAIGN PROMOTING A PRINTING COMPANY. **MEDIUM:** WAX, OIL, CRAYONS

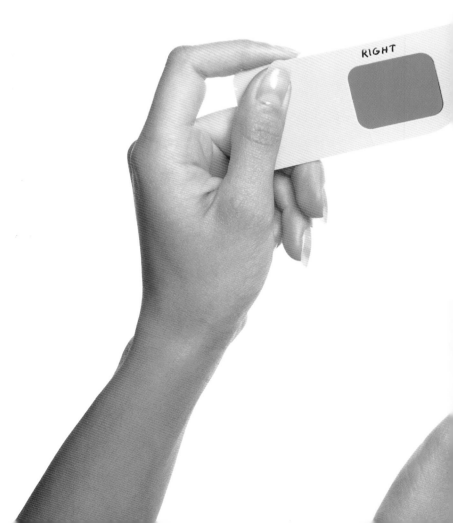

JONATHON ROSEN   **ART DIRECTOR:** STEPHEN BYRAM **CLIENT:** CBS RECORDS. A 3-D

MARKETING BROCHURE FOR PEOPLE WHO HAVE TO SELL RECORDS THAT DON'T SELL EASILY. **MEDIUM:** PEN & INK

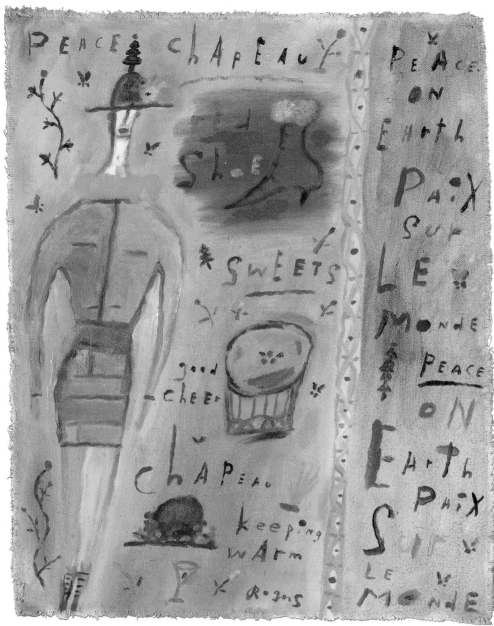

PUBLICATION: DETROIT MONTHLY MAGAZINE; DECEMBER 1989. AN ARTISTIC INTERPRETATION OF HOLIDAY FASHION. MEDIUM: PASTEL, GOUACHE, WATERCOLOR

LILLA ROGERS   ART DIRECTOR: AMY QUINLIVAN CLIENT: DAYTON HUDSON'S OVAL ROOM

CLIENT: GLENDALE GALLERIA; JUNE 1989 PUBLICATION: LOS ANGELES

TIMES. A FULL-PAGE ADVERTISEMENT FOR FATHER'S DAY GIFTS. MEDIUM: PEN AND INK, BRUSH WORK

ART DIRECTOR: BRENT CROXTON ADVERTISING AGENCY: ALTMAN & MANLEY

JESSIE HARTLAND

MEDIUM: INK, COLLAGE

STORE BANNERS FOR "SUMMER IN THE CITY" CAMPAIGN.

THOM SEVALRUD   ART DIRECTORS: NEIL FEDUN, DEBORAH DRUICK ADVERTISING AGENCY: SIMPSONS VISUAL PRESENTATION DEPARTMENT CLIENT: SIMPSONS DEPARTMENT STORE; APRIL 1989.

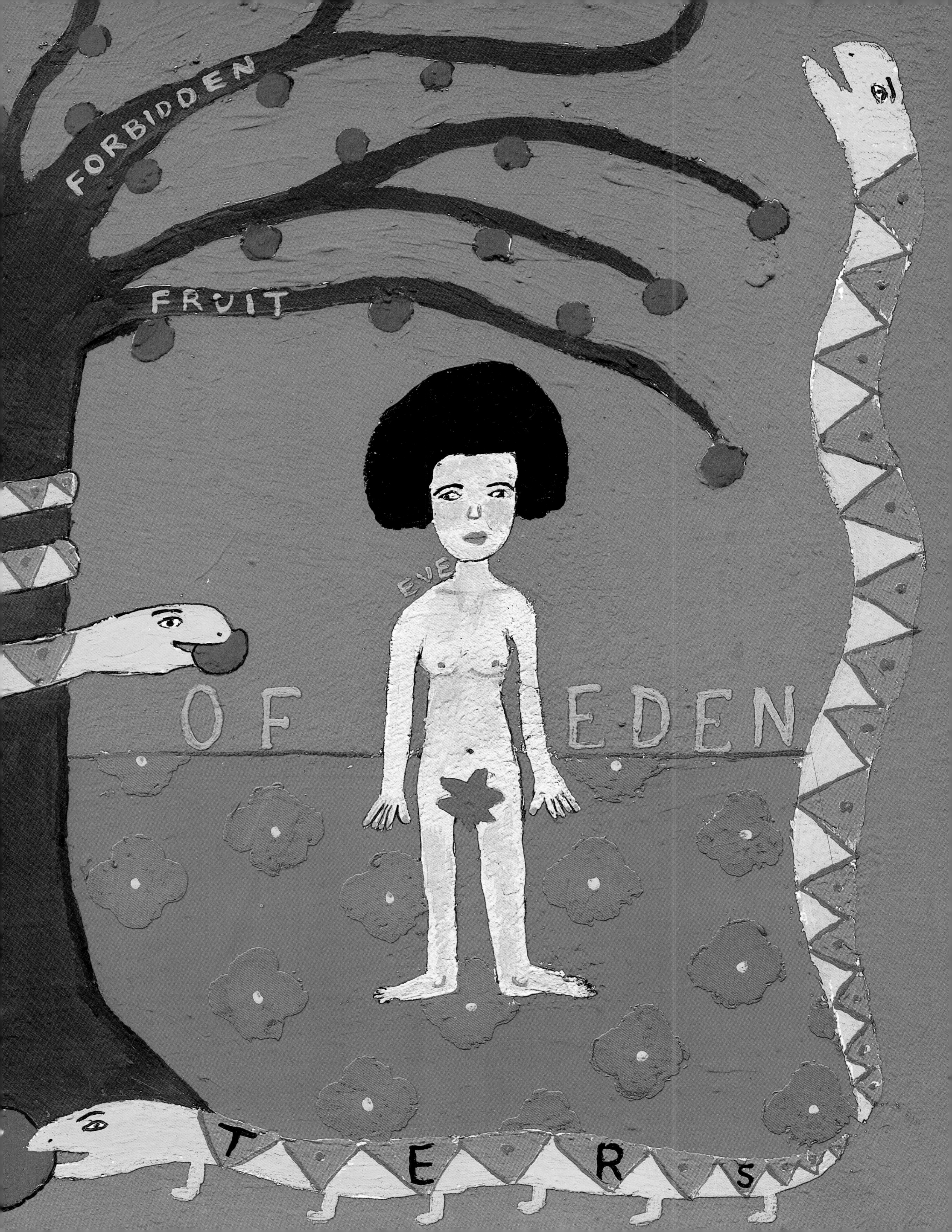
FORBIDDEN
FRUIT
EVE
OF
EDEN
TERs

JONATHON ROSEN **ART DIRECTOR:** JERI MCMANUS HEIDEN **CLIENT:** WARNER BROTHERS

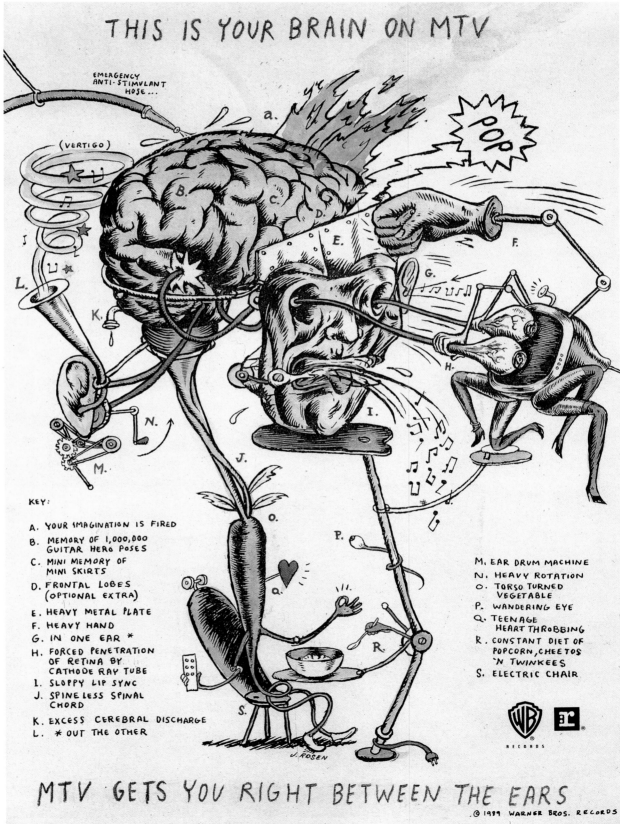

DON SIBLEY   **WRITER**: REX PETEET

MEDIUM: COMPUTER, INK, COLOR OVERLAYS

PHOTOGRAPHER: J.W. BURKEY **CLIENT**: GRAPHIC ARTISTS GROUP OF OMAHA; APRIL 1989. PROMOTIONAL POSTER TO ADVERTISE THE MONTHLY MEETING WITH GUEST SPEAKERS DON SIBLEY AND REX PETEET.

JENNIFER MORLA   **WRITER:** BRUCE BURDICK

CLIENT: STANFORD ALUMNI ASSOCIATION; MAY 1989. PROMOTIONAL POSTER FOR THE STANFORD CONFERENCE ON DESIGN DEPICTING THE GATHERING OF MEN AND WOMEN FROM ALL AREAS OF THE ARCHITECTURAL AND DESIGN PROFESSIONS. **MEDIUM:** PEN AND INK

CLIENT: RON REZEK LIGHTING AND FURNITURE, INC.: OCTOBER 1989 · A PROMOTIONAL POSTER FOR RON REZEK LIGHTING AND FURNITURE, INC. **MEDIUM:** SILKSCREEN

THE ARTS, BOSTON UNIVERSITY; NOVEMBER 1989. POSTER FOR THE PLAY, "THE MAN WHO CAME TO DINNER," PRODUCED BY THE BOSTON UNIVERSITY DRAMA DEPARTMENT. **MEDIUM:** MIXED MEDIA

JUDY FILIPPO **WRITER:** LORETTA CUBBERLEY **CLIENT:** SCHOOL FOR

POL TURGEON   **ART DIRECTOR:** JOSIANE POLIDORI **WRITER:** JOSIANE POLIDORI **CLIENT:** THE CANADA COUNCIL. WINTER 1990. PROMOTIONAL POSTER FOR THE NATIONAL BOOK FESTIVAL BASED ON THEIR SLOGAN "BOOK AN ADVENTURE." **MEDIUM:** MIXED MEDIA

CREATIVES, A DESIGN AND ADVERTISING AGENCY, INCORPORATING THEIR LIGHT BULB LOGO. **MEDIUM:** MIXED MEDIA

POL TURGEON   **ART DIRECTOR:** RICHARD VINCENT **WRITER:** CAMERON MILLER **CLIENT:** KUTOKA COMMUNICATIONS CREATIVES; WINTER 1990. PROMOTIONAL POSTER FOR KUTOKA COMMUNICATION

DEE ITO **ADVERTISING AGENCY:** SCHOOL OF VISUAL ARTS PRESS, LTD. **CLIENT:** SCHOOL OF VISUAL ARTS; SEPTEMBER 1989. PROMOTIONAL POSTER FOR THE SCHOOL OF VISUAL ARTS ILLUSTRATING THE PHRASE "AN IDEA IS ONLY AN IDEA UNTIL YOU MAKE IT REAL." **MEDIUM:** ACRYLIC

JERRY MORIARTY   **CREATIVE DIRECTOR:** SILAS RHODES **WRITER:**

-168-

CLIENTS: WATER MARK PRESS AND FRAZIER DESIGN. A PROMOTIONAL PIECE FOR WATER MARK PRESS AND FRAZIER DESIGN, CREATED FROM A 1-1/2 " STRIP OF TAPE. **MEDIUM:** BLACK MASKING TAPE

JON FLAMING   **ART DIRECTOR:** RON SULLIVAN **WRITER:** MARK PERKINS **ADVERTISING AGENCY:** SULLIVAN PERKINS **CLIENT:** DALLAS SOCIETY OF VISUAL COMMUNICATIONS; OCTOBER 1989.

INK, CLIP ART

INVITATION FOR ILLUSTRATOR STEVEN GUARNACCIA'S SPEAKING ENGAGEMENT AT THE DALLAS SOCIETY OF VISUAL COMMUNICATIONS, BASED ON A SKETCH BY GUARNACCIA. **MEDIUM:** WATERCOLOR, PEN AND

JIM MCMULLAN   **ART DIRECTOR:** NEAL POZNER **ADVERTISING AGENCY:** RUSSEK ADVERTISING **CLIENT:** LINCOLN CENTER THEATER; MAY 1989. PROMOTIONAL POSTER FOR THE SHAKESPEARE PLAY,

"MEASURE FOR MEASURE." **MEDIUM:** WATERCOLOR

PROMO.

AUGUST 1989. RECORD COVER FOR THIRD WORLD'S "IT'S THE SAME OLD SONG" ALBUM. **MEDIUM:** INK

MICHAEL KLOTZ   **ART DIRECTOR:** MARGERY GREENSPAN **CLIENT:** POLYGRAM RECORDS;

JUNE 1989. THIS PAINTED BOX HOLDS THE ARTIST'S PORTFOLIO. THE CASE HINTS AT ITS CONTENTS AND STANDS OUR AT DROP-OFF APPOINTMENTS. **MEDIUM:** ACRYLIC ON CARDBOARD

/7?

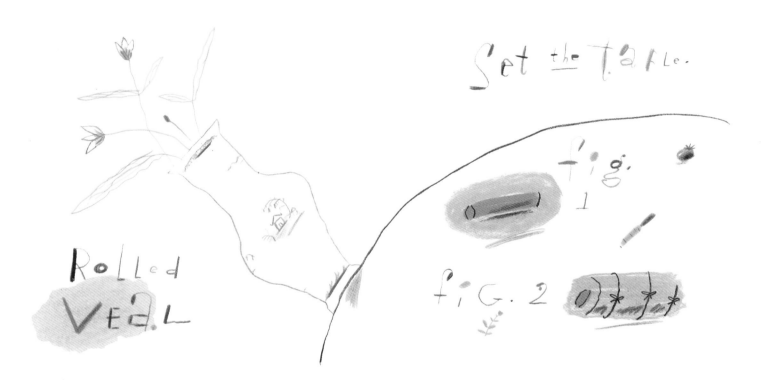

Set the T.a.b.Le.

Rolled Veal

fig. 1

fig. 2

17 8

DESIGN FIRM: SUSAN SLOVER DESIGN **CLIENT:** DONGHIA FURNITURE; JANUARY 1989. THIS QUIRKY COOKBOOK WAS USED AS A PROMOTIONAL GIFT FOR DONGHIA FURNITURE. **MEDIUM:** PASTEL, GOUACHE

fennel
chicken =

one chicken +

+ fennel   (root)

Rogers

179

Chocolate PASTA

4 level tablespoons

6 six servings / Add sauces.

FOR THIS SELF-PROMOTIONAL BOOK, FRAZIER USED BLACK MASKING TAPE TO CREATE ANIMAL ILLUSTRATIONS. **MEDIUM:** MASKING TAPE

monique

She had a plaid collar and I had a hat to match.

For Monique the language was NOT a problem.

Monique goes to Paris

her favorite stop

more plaid stuff

SELF-PROMOTIONAL PIECE. **MEDIUM:** WATERCOLOR

MARY LYNN BLASUTTA   MARCH 1990. A WHIMISCAL

NEIL SHIGLEY **ART DIRECTOR:** STACY DRUMMOND **CLIENT:** CBS RECORDS. PIANO KEYS IN DISARRAY SYMBOLIZE THE SHORT, TURBULENT LIFE OF BLUES PIANO PLAYER LEROY CARR. **MEDIUM:** WOODCUT

RECORD COVER FOR DAN HILL'S "REAL LOVE" ALBUM. **MEDIUM:** CHALK PASTEL

ANN FIELD   ART DIRECTOR: STACY DRUMMOND **CLIENT:** CBS RECORDS.

CLIENT: CBS RECORDS. A RECORD COVER FOR RUBY BRAFF'S ALL-STAR ALBUM. FRIEDMAN INCORPORATES JAZZ MUSIC AND THE CHAOTIC NEW YORK LIFESTYLE INTO THE DESIGN. **MEDIUM:** MIXED MEDIA

A Taste & a Toast

Westminster Hall

Baltimore, MD

11:30 am - 2:30 pm

Concert

ARTISTS

November 5 1989

185

DAVE PLUNKERT   **ART DIRECTOR:** TIM THOMPSON **WRITER:** CORDELIA OQRINZ

MUSIC, AND BALTIMORE'S GRITTY STREETS. **MEDIUM:** COLLAGE AND COMPUTER

DESIGN FIRM: GRAFFITO, INC. **PUBLISHER:** CONCERT ARTISTS OF BALTIMORE; FALL 1989. INVITATION AND PROGRAM COVER FOR THE EVENT "A TASTE AND A FEAST." THE PIECE COMBINES IMAGES OF FOOD,

187

ART DIRECTOR: STEPHEN BYRAM **CLIENT:** CBS RECORDS. RECORD COVER FOR AHMAD JAMAL'S "POINCIANA" ALBUM. **MEDIUM:** MIXED MEDIA

STEPHEN KRONINGER

CLIENT: CBS RECORDS. RECORD COVER FOR SLAMMIN WATUSIS'S "KING OF NOISE" ALBUM. **MEDIUM:** MIXED MEDIA

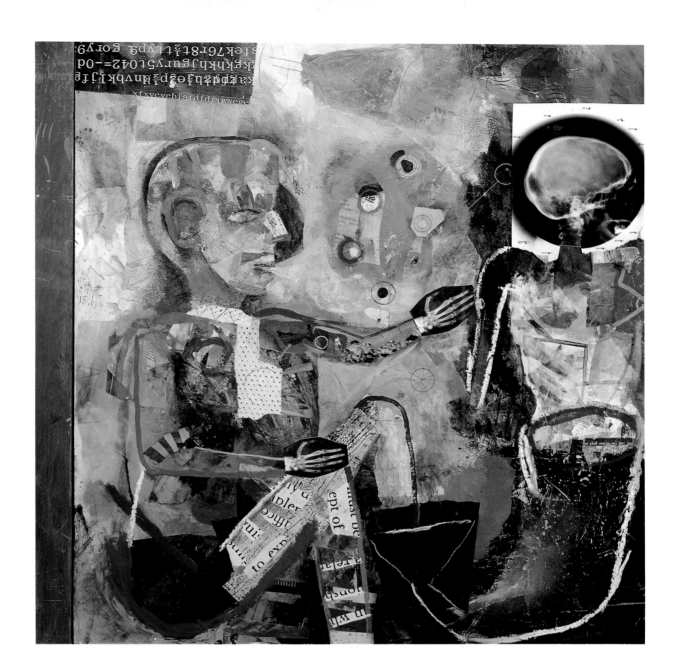

189

197

PETER KUPER   JANUARY 1989. A PROMOTIONAL PIECE THAT ANNOUNCED THE ARTIST WAS OFF ON A

PHILIPPE WEISBECKER

ART DIRECTOR: ROBERT VALENTINE **CLIENT:** BLOOMINGDALE'S; SUMMER 1989. ILLUSTRATION FOR THE SUMMER 1989 SHOPPING BAG FOR BLOOMINGDALE'S. **MEDIUM:** PEN AND INK, WATERCOLOR

192

ART DIRECTOR: SCOTT WADLER; NOVEMBER 1989. PROMOTIONAL MAILER ANNOUNCING THE EXHIBITION OF WARREN LINN'S WORK, HIS LECTURE, AND WORKSHOP. **MEDIUM:** SCRATCHBOARD, COLLAGE

193

WARREN LINN

ANNUAL REPORT. **MEDIUM:** MIXED MEDIA, COLLAGE

GENE GREIF   ART DIRECTOR: PETER HARRISON **DESIGNER:** HAROLD BURCH **DESIGN FIRM:** PENTAGRAM DESIGN **PUBLISHER:** WARNER COMMUNICATIONS. A SPREAD FROM WARNER COMMUNICATIONS' 1989

volume **one** issue three

JUNK FAX
magazine

FEATUREING:

SKETCHBOOK

europe in 1992 & HOW TO GIT IN.
*Marketing Communication mag cover —
Lynn Rover a.d.*

LIST OF WORDS ?

Kampeuchea burma

ATLAS

Co Cambodia
Madagascar - Rongo

*renaming Countries : INA SALTZ
art director Time magazine*

*fallable Technology : Newsweek Cover SKETCH
for Patricia Bradbury*

*new government industry regulations
BUSINESS WEEK for Louise White*

196

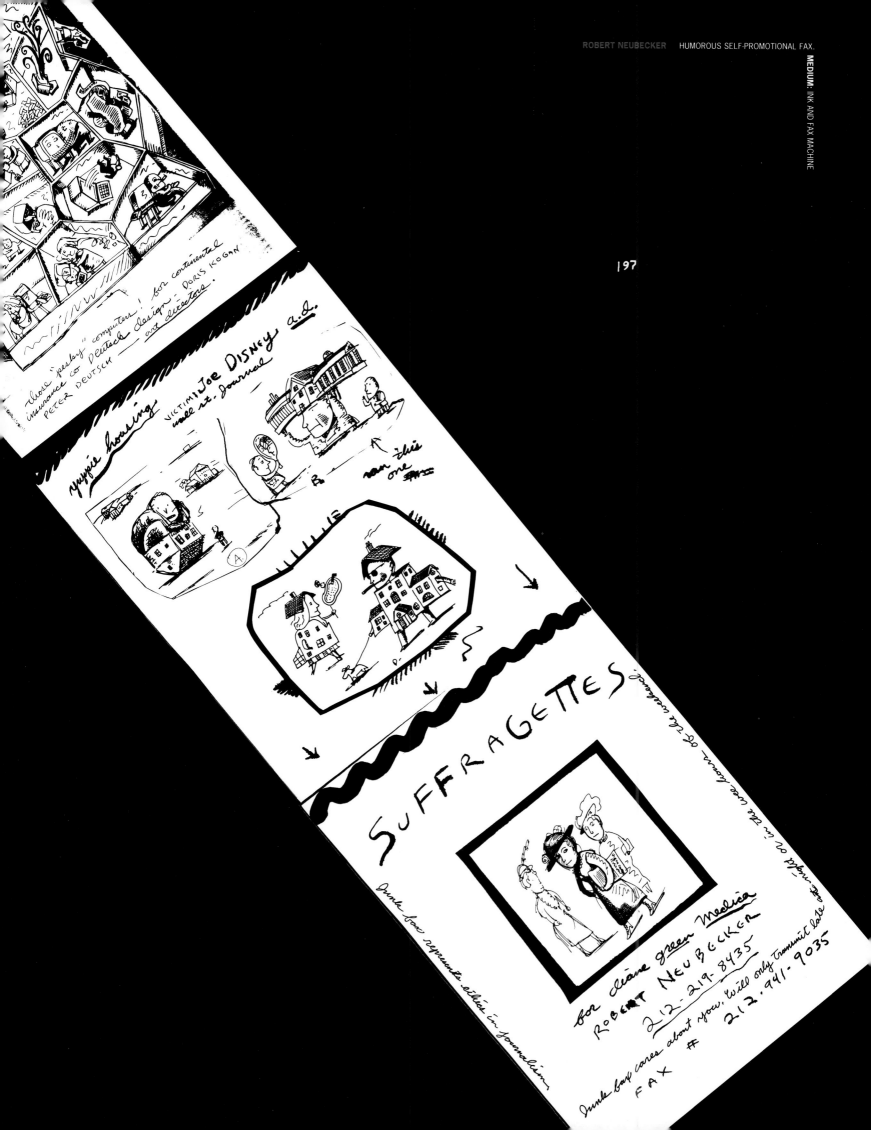

198

ANDERS WENNGREN   SELF-PROMOTIONAL MAILER.   **MEDIUM:** SILKSCREEN

MEDIUM: ACRYLIC ON SHIRT CARDBOARD.

PAUL DAVIS   **DESIGN FIRM:** PAUL DAVIS STUDIO; DECEMBER 1989. CHRISTMAS CARD FOR PAUL DAVIS STUDIO.

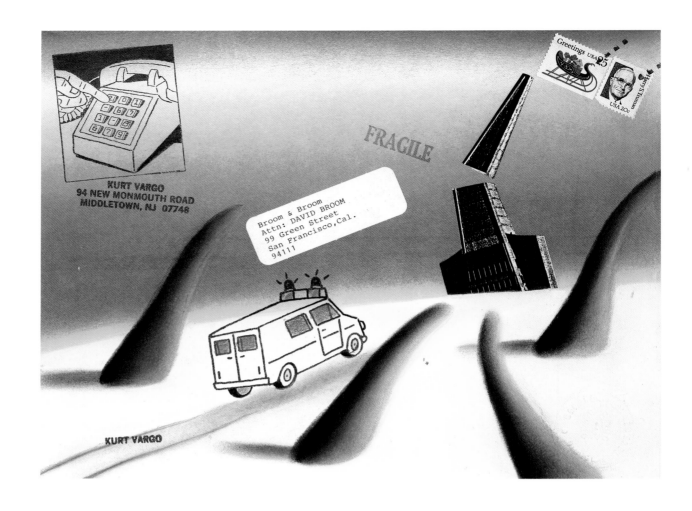

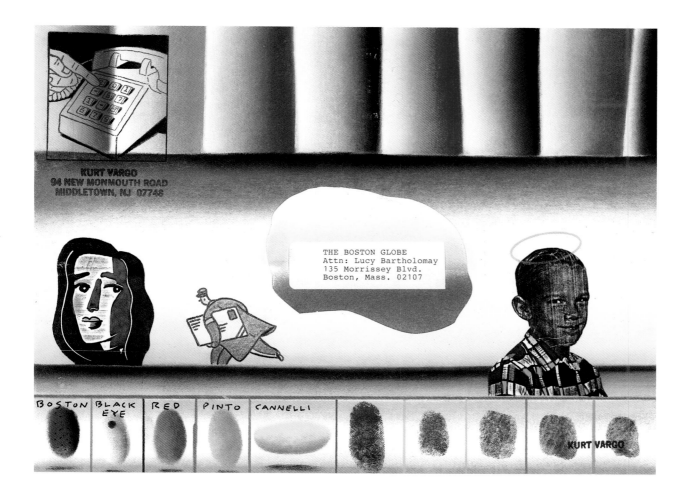

WINTER 1989. THIS ILLUSTRATED ENVELOPE WAS USED AS A SELF-PROMOTIONAL PIECE. **MEDIUM:** COLLAGE, RUBBER STAMPS, GOUACHE, NU-PASTELS

KURT VARGO **ART DIRECTOR:** JAMES SEBASTIAN **DESIGNER:** MARGARET WOLLENHAUPT **WRITER:** RALPH CAPLAN **DESIGN FIRM:** DESIGNFRAME INC. **CLIENT:** THE HILLER GROUP/SIMPSON PAPER CO. THIS PROMOTIONAL ENVELOPE CONTAINED A BROCHURE FOR SIMPSON PAPER CO. IN

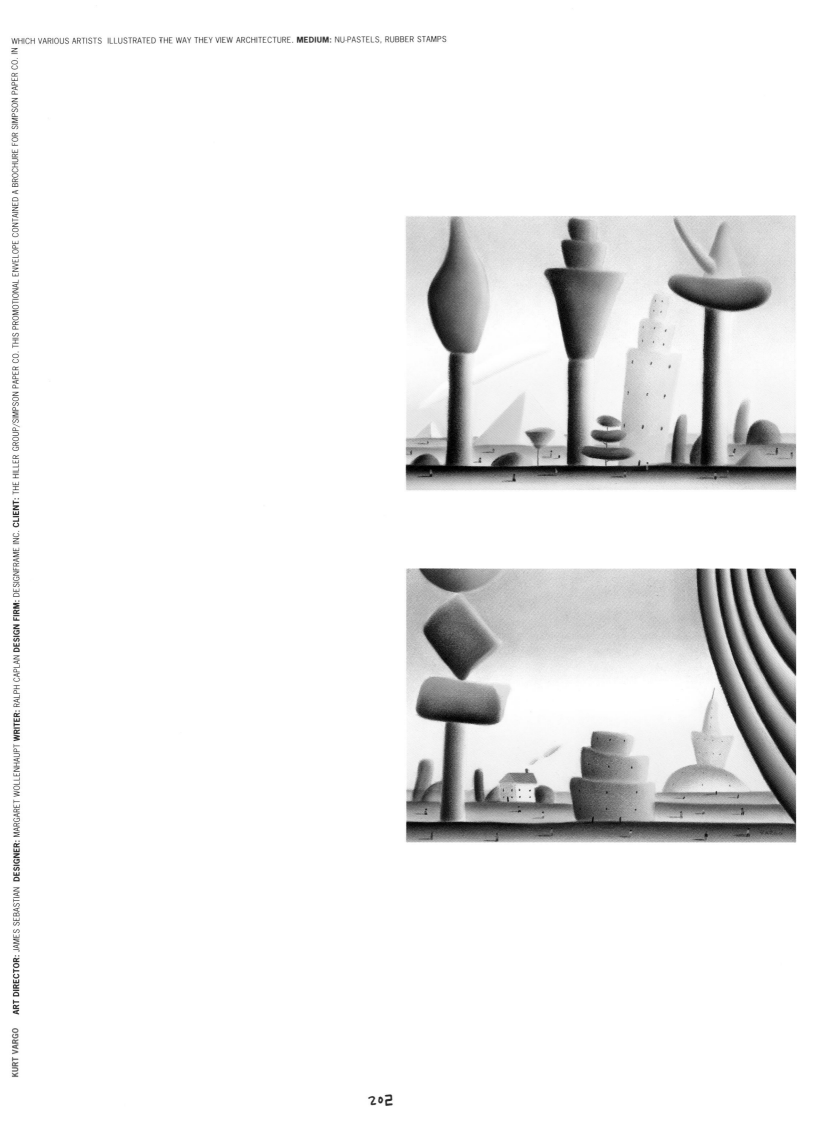

NICHOLAS VITACCO **PUBLISHER:** RENO ART WORKS; FALL 1989. SELF-PROMOTIONAL

204

PIECE USED BY THE ARTIST'S REPRESENTATIVE AGENCY. **MEDIUM:** CEL-VINYL ON ACETATE

CLIENT: WARNER BROTHERS (REPRISE RECORDS); DECEMBER 1989. CHRISTMAS CARD FOR WARNER BROTHERS'S REPRISE RECORDS DIVISION. **MEDIUM:** PEN AND INK, WATERCOLOR

MEDIUM: OIL ON PHOTOGRAPH

206

AMY GUIP   **ART DIRECTOR:** RIA LEWERKE **CLIENT:** RCA RECORDS. ALBUM COVER FOR A RECORD BY THE BAND "GYPSY ROSE."

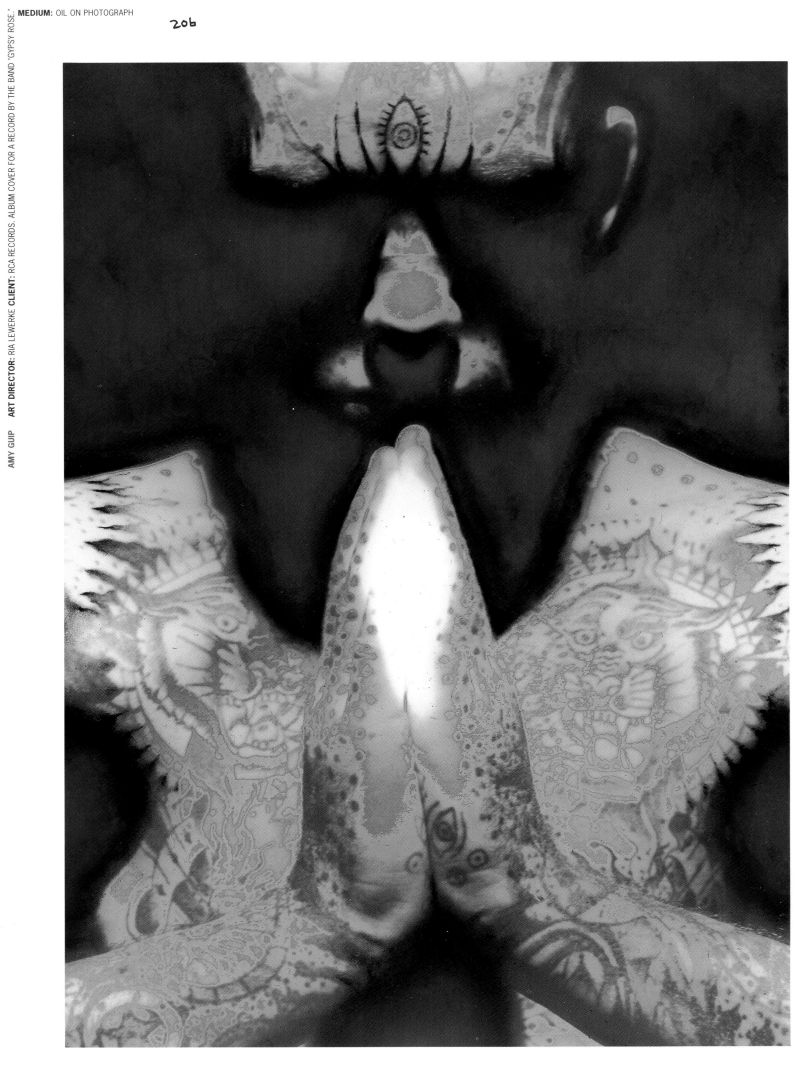

AN ILLUSTRATION FOR A SUMMER T-SHIRT FOR THE COMPANY PICNIC. SUMMER 1989.

CHRIS LYONS   **DESIGNER:** CHRIS LYONS   **CLIENT:** BUCK & PULLEYN ADVERTISING AGENCY;

CLEMENT MOK   **ART DIRECTOR:** CLEMENT MOK   **PUBLICATION:** AIGA TECHNOLOGY EXPLORITORIUM PROGRAM OF EVENTS   **PUBLISHING COMPANY:**

AIGA; OCTOBER 1989. AN ILLUSTRATION EXPRESSING HOW TECHNOLOGY IS INFLUENCING ART AND DESIGN. **MEDIUM:** COMPUTER

208

NANCY KLOBUCAR   **ART DIRECTOR:** TATSUOMI MAJIMA **DESIGN FIRM:** MAJIMA DESIGN INC. **PUBLISHER:** GULLIVER BOOK CO., LTD; JANUARY 1990. ILLUSTRATIONS FOR A 1990 CALENDAR.

THE IMAGES REFLECT THE ARTIST'S LOVE OF PORTRAITURE. **MEDIUM:** ACRYLIC ON CANVAS

ANTHONY RUSSO   **ART DIRECTOR:** MARIE DUSAULT

PUBLISHER: DNP AMERICA. ILLUSTRATION INSPIRED BY AN ERIK SATIE PIECE USED IN A 1990 DAI NIPPON CALENDAR. **MEDIUM:** ACRYLIC

NEW

211

DESIGN. **MEDIUM:** INK, PASTEL

ETTY YANIV **DESIGNER:** JUDY FENDELMAN **PUBLISHER:** PARSONS SCHOOL OF DESIGN, ILLUSTRATION DEPARTMENT; APRIL 1989. AN INVITATION FOR THE SENIOR STUDENTS EXHIBIT AT PARSONS SCHOOL OF

EDGAR SOBERON   JANUARY 1989. IMAGES DEPICTING "POUNDING THE PAVEMENT," WERE USED AS A SELF-PROMOTIONAL PIECE FOR THE ILLUSTRATOR. **MEDIUM:** PASTELS, PENCILS

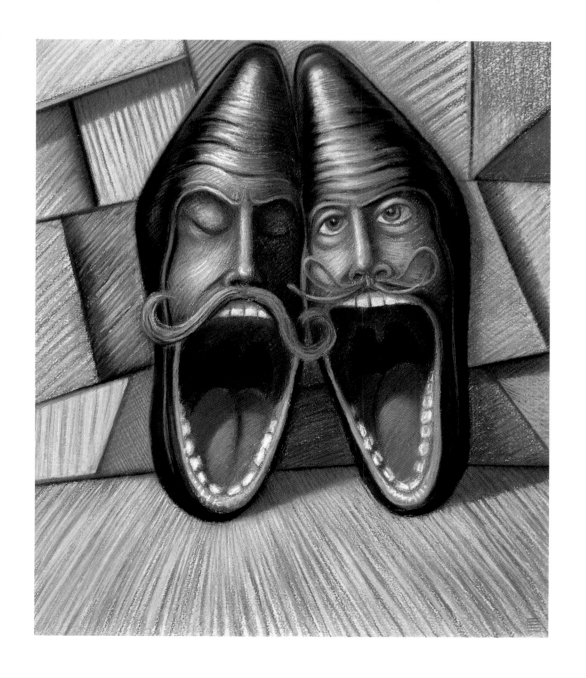

214

MICHAEL BARTALOS OCTOBER 1989. SELF-PROMOTIONAL POSTCARD ANNOUNCING THE ARTIST'S RETURN TO NEW YORK FROM TOKYO ON HALLOWEEN.

MAPS
&

CHARTS

ROSS MACDONALD   **ART DIRECTOR:** FRED WOODWARD **DESIGNER:** CATHERINE GILMORE-BARNES **PUBLICATION:** ROLLING STONE **PUBLISHER:** STRAIGHT ARROW PUBLISHERS; JULY 1989. MACDONALD WAS ASKED TO DRAW A MAP THAT SHOWS THE FAVORITE SUMMER HANG-OUTS OF SOME PROMINENT POP STARS. **MEDIUM:** MIXED MEDIA

unPublished

KAREN BARBOUR FEBRUARY 1990.

A PERSONAL PIECE, BASED ON THE EXPERIENCES OF A FRIEND IN A BAR. **MEDIUM:** GOUACHE

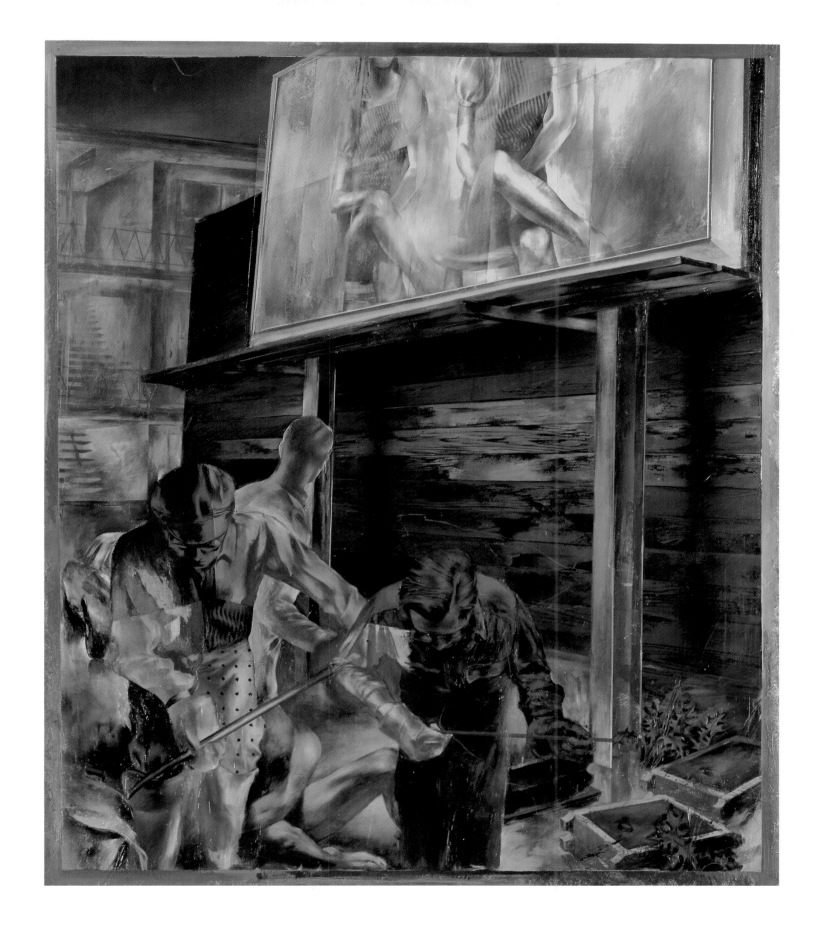

DAVID RYAN "ALAMEDA" · FALL 1989

THESE PAINTINGS WERE INSPIRED BY LOCATIONS IN ALAMEDA, AN ISLAND TOWN IN CALIFORNIA WHERE RYAN GREW UP. **MEDIUM:** ACRYLIC

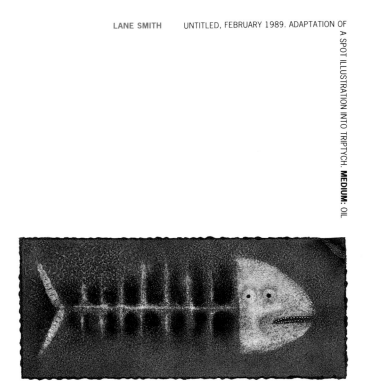

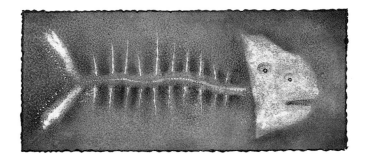

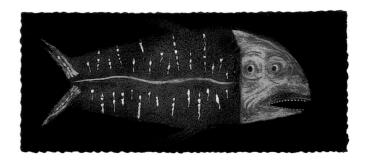

LANE SMITH

ART DIRECTOR: TERESA FERNANDES. UNTITLED, AUGUST 1989. A PIECE ON THE SUBJECT OF NUCLEAR ENERGY. SMITH FEELS COLLAGE LENT ITSELF BEST TO THE EXPRESSION OF TURMOIL. **MEDIUM:** MIXED MEDIA

AMY GUIP   UNTITLED, OCTOBER 1989. FOR THIS PERSONAL PIECE, GUIP COMBINED TWO NEGATIVES AND USED SEVERAL TYPES OF TONER. THE PHOTO IMAGE WAS PAINTED OVER WITH OIL. **MEDIUM:** PHOTOGRAPHY, OIL

PEOPLE IN OUR LIVES. **MEDIUM:** SCRATCHBOARD, COLLAGE, OIL PASTELS

"ARTIST WITH ANNUNCIATION," JUNE 1989 • AN ARTIST WITH THE VIRGIN MARY ON HIS MIND. **MEDIUM:** MIXED MEDIA

237

SERGIO BARADAT   **TITLE:** "LITTLE EGYPT", JUNE 1989. AN ILLUSTRATION OF

UNTITLED, 1989. IMAGE OF DEPECHE MODE IN CONCERT AT THE ROSE BOWL IN PASADENA, CALIFORNIA. **MEDIUM:** CHARCOAL, PASTEL

THESSY MEHRAIN

"WHAT'S ON A WOMAN'S MIND?," DECEMBER 1989. THIS IMAGE IS AN UPDATE ON THE ARTIST'S STATE OF MIND. **MEDIUM:** GOUACHE

RUTH MARTEN

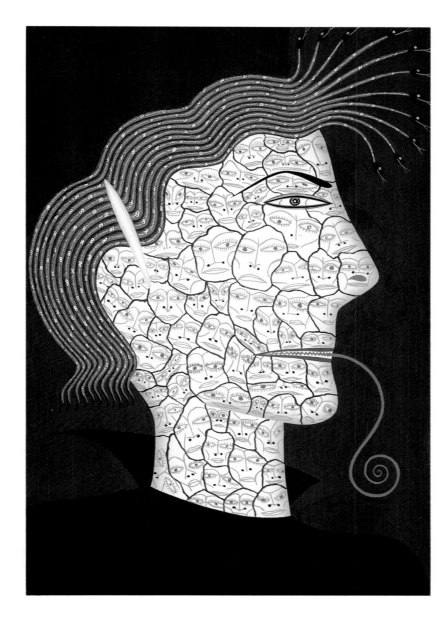

RUTH MARTEN UNTITLED, OCTOBER 1988. AN INTRIGUING IMAGE FROM THE PERSONAL BOOK ON ANGELS AND DEVILS, DEALING WITH THE MANY VOICES WITHIN. **MEDIUM:** GOUACHE AND EGG SOLUTION ON WOOD

RUTH MARTEN UNTITLED, OCTOBER 1988. A PERSONAL WORK FOR A BOOK ON ANGELS AND DEVILS, FOCUSING ON THE INTERNAL BATTLE OF THE SEXES. **MEDIUM:** GOUACHE

GARY BASEMAN · "A DAY IN THE LIFE." · DECEMBER 1989. CREATED FOR THE "ILLUSTRATED DOG" SHOW AT THE ILLUSTRATION GALLERY. **MEDIUM:** ACRYLIC

GARY BASEMAN UNTITLED, SEPTEMBER 1989.

GARY BASEMAN   "DEVIL DOG," DECEMBER 1989.   CREATED FOR THE "ILLUSTRATED DOG" SHOW AT THE ILLUSTRATION GALLERY.

MEDIUM: PASTELS & ACRYLIC

247

ETTY YANIV   UNTITLED, SEPTEMBER 1989. A PERSONAL WORK

PAINTED FROM A DRAWING OF A MODEL. **MEDIUM:** MIXED MEDIA

SAM TOMASELLO "EAST VILLAGE PIZZA MANIA," AUGUST 1989. A PERSONAL PIECE DONE IN RESPONSE TO THE QUALITY AND POPULARITY OF PIZZA IN NEW YORK CITY. **MEDIUM:** CHARCOAL PENCILS

260

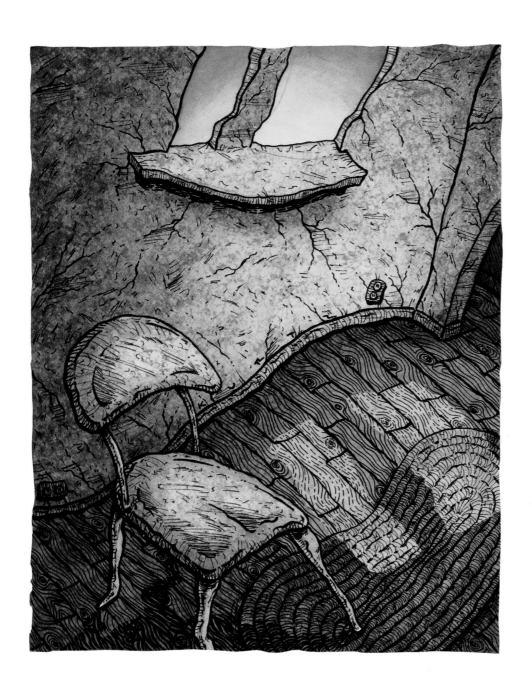

KEVIN KURTZ UNTITLED, DECEMBER 1989. A PERSONAL

PIECE SHOWS THE MENACING EFFECT OF TOXIC SPILLS, RADIATION, ETC. **MEDIUM:** WATERCOLOR, CRAYON, COLLAGE

MICHELLE BARNES   "MARITAL DIFFICULTIES," JUNE 1989. **MEDIUM:** INK, CRAYON RESIST, PASTEL

now Bob can go to parties and not have to say a thing.

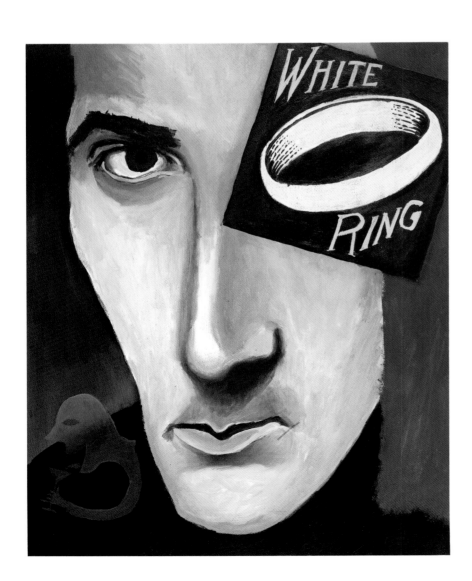

JOSH GOSFIELD   " WYNONIE HARRIS," 1989.

MICHAEL THIBODEAU UNTITLED. MARCH 1989. ONE OF EIGHT PAINTINGS FOR A THESIS PROJECT (SCHOOL OF VISUAL ARTS). **MEDIUM: PASTEL**

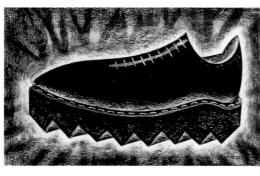

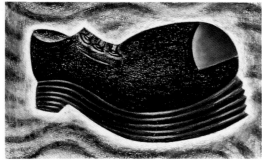

MARY LYNN BLASUTTA   FEBRUARY 1990. TIE AND JACKET, A SELF PROMOTIONAL MAILER. **MEDIUM:** INDIA INK

CALEF BROWN   "TWO SHOES." OCTOBER 1989. INSPIRED BY BROWN'S FIANCEE'S COLLECTION OF FOOTWEAR. **MEDIUM:** PASTELS

JESSIE HARTLAND   " BLUE PLATE SPECIAL,"

STEVEN GUARNACCIA   "NOSEDIVE BOWL-A-RAMA," NOVEMBER 1989. ONE OF MANY PIECES EXHIBITED AT THE REACTOR GALLERY IN TORONTO, EACH USING A FOUND SURFACE

AND VARIOUS OBJECTS TO MAKE A FACE. **MEDIUM:** WOODEN BOWL, ACRYLIC PAINT

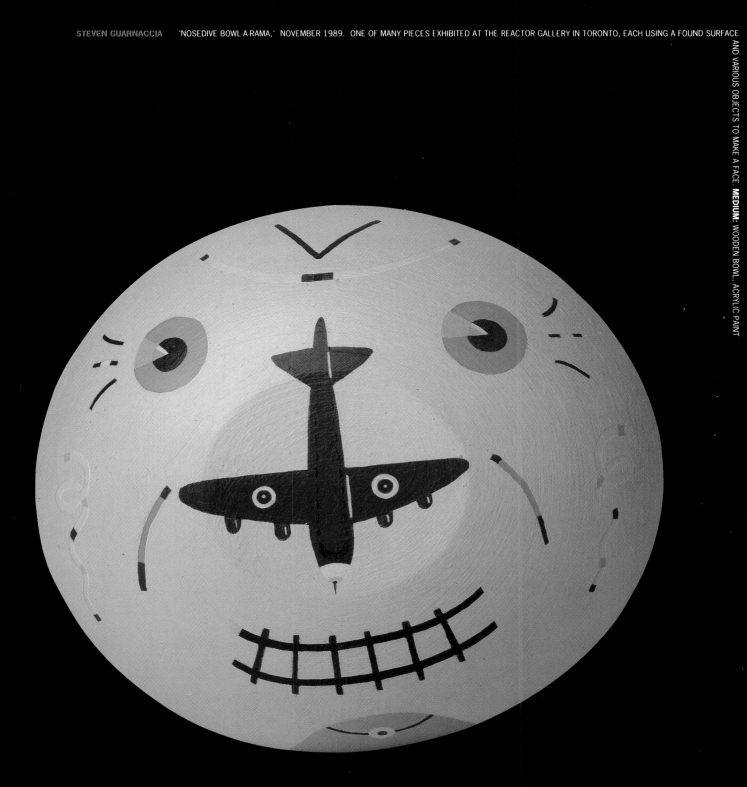

EVERETT PECK " JUST GOOD FRIENDS." FEBRUARY 1989. A PERSONAL PIECE DEALING WITH LOVE, ROMANCE, AND RELATED PROBLEMS. **MEDIUM:** ACRYLIC

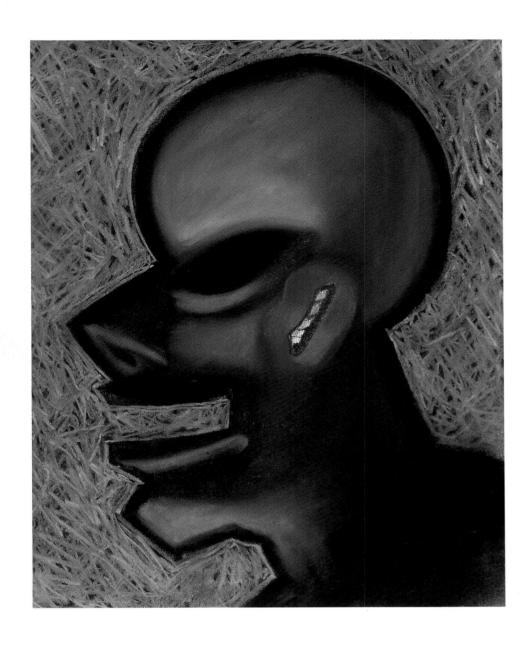

OUR FEELINGS. **MEDIUM:** PASTELS

MEDIUM: INK, WATERCOLOR, GOUACHE

TOM BACHTELL "CABARET SINGER," JANUARY 1990.

ALISON MORITSUGU "CHINATOWN, NEW YORK," DECEMBER 1989. A PERSONAL PIECE BASED ON LOCATION SKETCHES MADE IN NEW YORK'S CHINATOWN. **MEDIUM:** MIXED MEDIA

"ACID IS FLACCID," SUMMER 1989. WALES' ANTI-DRUG PIECE ASKS KIDS TO CHOOSE A TRIP TO THE ZOO RATHER THAN A TRIP ON ACID. **MEDIUM:** GOUACHE, LASER COPIER

DAVID ART WALES

285

287

TWO PERSONAL PIECES WHICH EVOLVED DURING THEIR CREATION.

THIS DRAWING WAS MADE AFTER A WALK THROUGH CHINATOWN DURING A HEAT WAVE. **MEDIUM:** PEN AND INK, WATERCOLOR

GARY BASEMAN "BEWARE OF PLAID DOG," DECEMBER 1989. CREATED FOR THE "ILLUSTRATED DOG" SHOW AT THE ILLUSTRATION GALLERY. **MEDIUM:** PASTELS

BASEMAN

film (film) *n.* 1. A thin skin

FILM

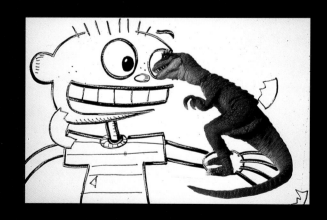

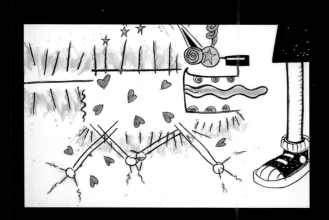

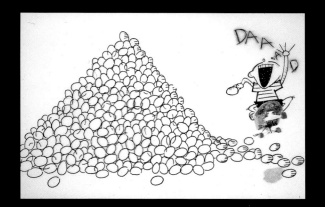

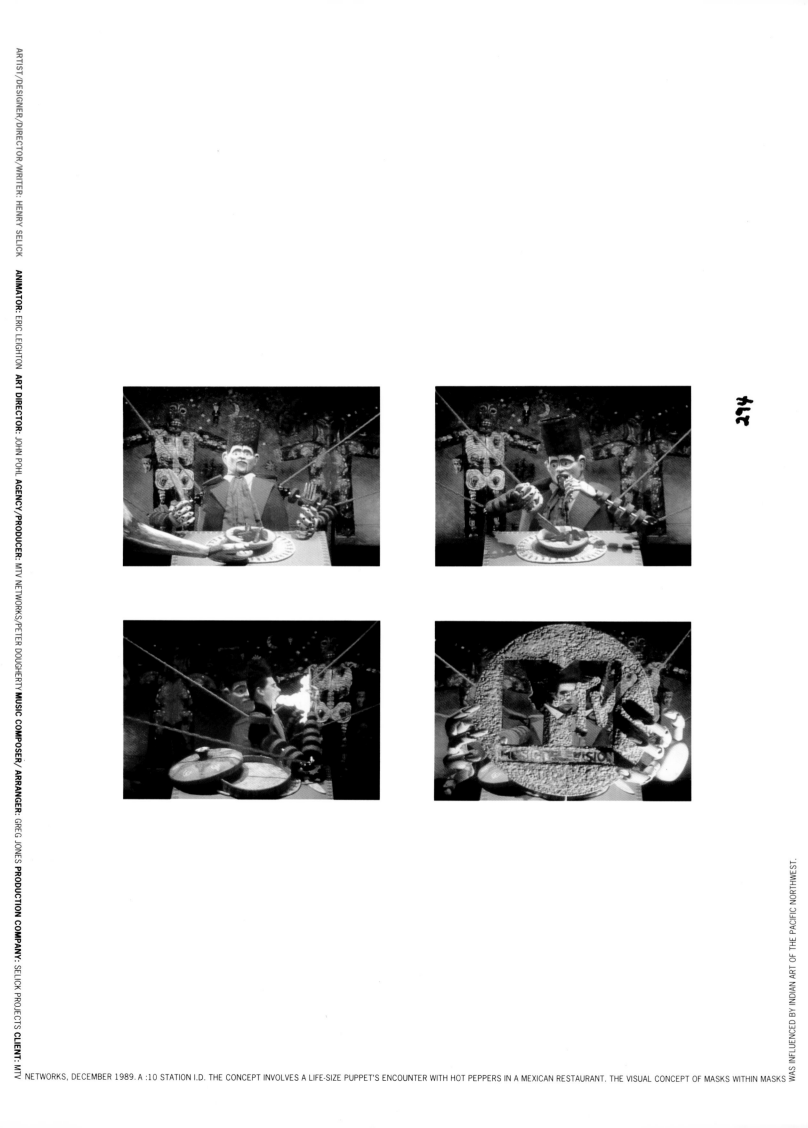

ARTIST/DESIGNER/DIRECTOR/WRITER: HENRY SELICK **ANIMATOR:** ERIC LEIGHTON **ART DIRECTOR:** JOHN POHL **AGENCY/PRODUCER:** MTV NETWORKS/PETER DOUGHERTY **MUSIC COMPOSER/ ARRANGER:** GREG JONES **PRODUCTION COMPANY:** SELICK PROJECTS **CLIENT:** MTV

NETWORKS, DECEMBER 1989. A :10 STATION I.D. THE CONCEPT INVOLVES A LIFE-SIZE PUPPET'S ENCOUNTER WITH HOT PEPPERS IN A MEXICAN RESTAURANT. THE VISUAL CONCEPT OF MASKS WITHIN MASKS WAS INFLUENCED BY INDIAN ART OF THE PACIFIC NORTHWEST.

ARTIST/DESIGNER:DOUGLAS FRASER **ANIMATORS:** COLOSSAL PICTURES **DIRECTOR:** MICHAEL BRUSFELD **WRITER:** DAVE MERHAR **ART DIRECTOR:** MATT CANZANO **AGENCY/PRODUCER:** J.WALTER THOMPSON

MARTYN LAURENCE **MUSIC COMPOSER/ARRANGER:** TULLIO & RANS **PRODUCTION COMPANY:** COLOSSAL PICTURES **CLIENT:** MILLER BREWING COMPANY , NOVEMBER 1989. FOR THIS :30 TV COMMERCIAL

FOR MILLER BREWING COMPANY, DESIGNER DOUGLAS FRASER COMBINED BOLD IMAGES WITH GRACEFUL COMPOSITION.

296

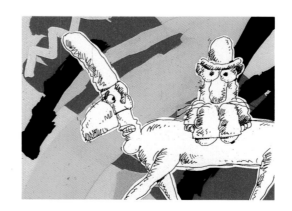

DOUGHERTY **MUSIC COMPOSER/ARRANGER:** BUTTHOLE SURFERS **PRODUCTION COMPANY:** SELICK PROJECTS **CLIENT:** MTV NETWORKS, AUGUST 1989. THIS :25 ANIMATION WAS CREATED FOR MTV'S TOP OF THE HOUR I.D. ARTIST HENRY SELICK DESIGNED THIS INTENSE PIECE WITH THE HELP OF 3-D MODELS, THE MACINTOSH COMPUTER, AND THE QUANTEL HARRY.

ARTIST/DESIGNER/DIRECTOR: **HENRY SELICK** **ANIMATOR:** ERIC LEIGHTON **ART DIRECTORS:** RON DAVIS, TED SOMOGYI **AGENCY/ PRODUCER:** MTV NETWORKS/PETER

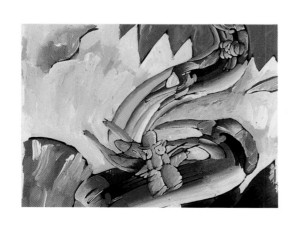

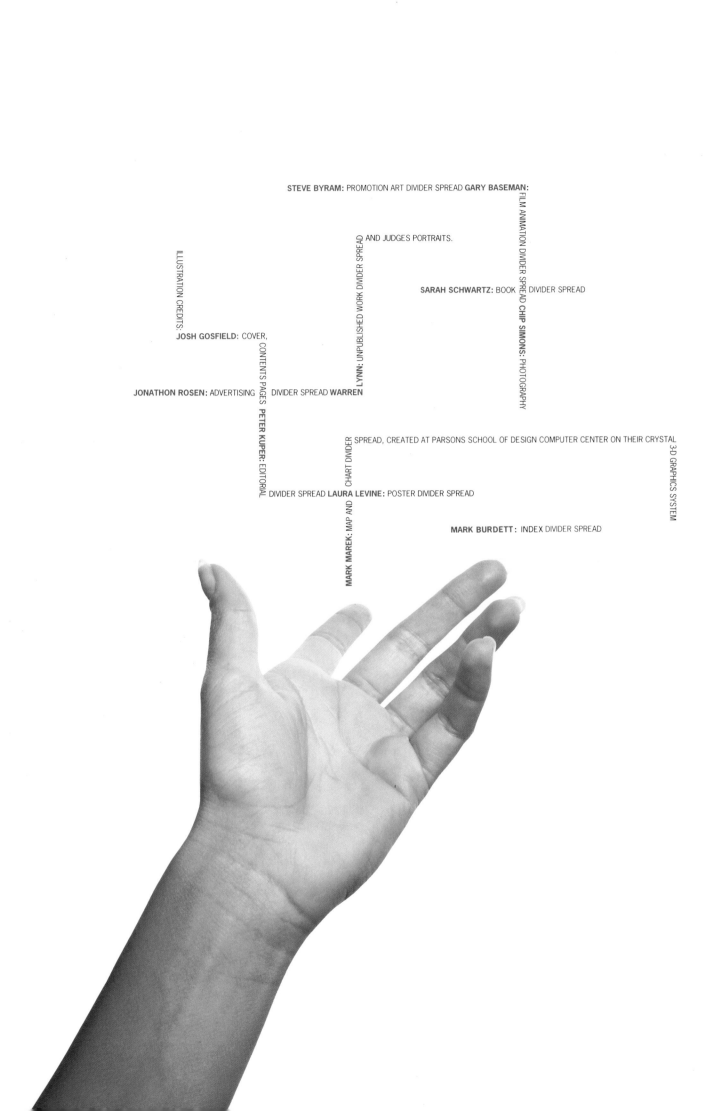

ILLUSTRATION CREDITS:

STEVE BYRAM: PROMOTION ART DIVIDER SPREAD GARY BASEMAN: FILM ANIMATION DIVIDER SPREAD

AND JUDGES PORTRAITS.

SARAH SCHWARTZ: BOOK DIVIDER SPREAD CHIP SIMONS: PHOTOGRAPHY

JOSH GOSFIELD: COVER, CONTENTS PAGES

LYNN: UNPUBLISHED WORK DIVIDER SPREAD

JONATHON ROSEN: ADVERTISING DIVIDER SPREAD WARREN

PETER KUPER: EDITORIAL

MARK MAREK: MAP AND CHART DIVIDER SPREAD, CREATED AT PARSONS SCHOOL OF DESIGN COMPUTER CENTER ON THEIR CRYSTAL 3-D GRAPHICS SYSTEM

DIVIDER SPREAD LAURA LEVINE: POSTER DIVIDER SPREAD

MARK BURDETT: INDEX DIVIDER SPREAD